# Primitive  Benchmark
## A Short Treatise on a
## General Theory of Sailing
## with the Limits
## for Sailboat Speed

# Primitive Benchmark
## A Short Treatise on a General Theory of Sailing with the Limits for Sailboat Speed

Jerry N. Selness

Windward Enterprises
WEGT Publishing
San Diego, California

Publisher's Cataloging-in-Publication
(Provided by Quality Books, Inc.)

Selness, Jerry N.
    Primitive benchmark : a short treatise on a
general theory of sailing with the limits of
sailboat speed / Jerry N. Selness. - - 1st ed.
        P. cm.
    Includes bibliographical references and index.
    ISBN: 0-9671566-0-2

    1. Sailing- -Mathematical models.  2. Sailing- -
Aerodynamics.  3. Invariants.  4. Convergence.
5. Yachting.  I. Title.

VK545.S45 1999                    623.8'223
                            QBI99-1134

First Edition

Published by
Windward Enterprises
WEGT Publishing
San Diego, California

Edited by Robert H. Watrous
Cover by Peter Horjus
Typesetting by Terry Hertzler
Printed in the United States of America

LCCN 99-95091
ISBN 0-9671566-0-2

# Table of Contents

Page

# Preface

This treatise is written for the thirsty-open-minded and the plain-open-minded reader. It is written for those thirsty for new-edge knowledge, new understandings. This is written for open-minded yachtsmen and yachtswomen of the sea and yachtsmen and yachtswomen of ideas, sailmakers, naval architects, mathematicians, physicists, biologists, engineers, sailors, antiquarians, philosophers and historians, voyagers on the seas of understanding—all these persons are for whom this is written. It is written by a simple seeker of truth for seekers of truths. It is written to convey hard-fought-for understandings of an object that lives in the wind and is propelled to ride on or plough the seas: the sailboat object. Discoveries are written about that advance the understanding of the sailboat phenomena in life, both past and present. The theory presented is general. While wrought for the sailboat object of nature, it can have applications in fields outside the sailboat.

There are people to thank for their help during the theory's initial development. Doug Deeds is to be thanked for listening while I was testing the theory and suggesting that I add appendage resistance to specific boat tests when testing the theory's ability to predict specific boat speeds. Gino Morilli is to be thanked for providing specific boat-measured data in two winds for *General Data*, a Formula 40 cat. The data was used to calibrate appendage frontal area-to-pound displacement for appendage resistance that made initial predictions exact for *General Data*. The resulting frontal area-to-pound displacement was reasonable for structural requirements of the appendage, making that initial independent test result a big boost in confidence in the theory. Eric Bylaska (Ph.D., Physical Chemistry) produced *RAWF* charts for an independent check of the author's originally produced charts. Dr. Nolan Wallach (Professor of Mathematics, UCSD) reviewed the chapter on theorems.

I wish to thank editor Robert H. Watrous, whose focus provided necessary tightening of the manuscript. And I wish to thank Ila Keefer for typing Chapter 12.

I am grateful for a Helen Hawkins Research Grant from the San Diego Independent Scholars which helped in the completion of the manuscript.

Georgs Kolesnikovs is to be thanked for holding the speed sailing events in Long Beach, California, just before completing his quest to beat *Flying Cloud's* long standing coast-to-coast, rounding-Cape-Horn passage record, by sailing his multihull boat, *Great American*. Surprising race results I witnessed, from two different boats (*Aikane and Beowulf*) at the speed sailing events, started me thinking and rethinking my understanding of the sailboat. The rethinking eventually led to the general theory. Don Hyslop, Chuck Cheyney, and Roger Grant are to be thanked for commissioning polar charts for their sailboats, which were done using the theory.

For those who read this, I trust it will increase and advance their understanding of the sailboats they observe, sail, and admire, whether they be on the water or in their minds.

# Chapter 1 - Introduction

New ideas, concepts, and understandings regarding "the sailboat" as an object, a phenomena of nature, are the focus of the chapters in this treatise. This work is precious to the reader who grasps the new understandings and ponders their content. Parts of the ideas are built on a foundation of concepts traceable and attributable to previous thinkers. They begin with the fundamental ideas of Pythagoras and Euclid along with those of Archimedes. Many concepts that make up the foundation for the theory preexisted the general theory, but the thought experiment beginning the thinking that just preceded the theory, was on "a blank page." An example of an imaginary thought experiment in the history of mathematics that led to a theory is the definition that $i = \sqrt{-1}$.

The general theory describes the sailboat as an object. It is not an aerodynamic theory, nor is it a hydrodynamic theory. The general theory does use aerodynamic and hydrodynamic information, however. It also makes the information in such recent monumental works as Marchaj's *Aero-Hydrodynamics of Sailing* (1979) or Hoerner's *Fluid Dynamic Drag* (1965) more useful to yachtsmen and yachtswomen, sailmakers, and naval architects.

The theory and its results, while partly based on traditional concepts, are nontraditional, nonconventional. A sailboat's motion is the result of various forces acting upon it in a kind of yin and yang balance that defines the equilibrium motion of a sailboat. Recent research and writings on naval architecture emphasize the yang part of a sailboat's motion, the responding and resisting forces. The general theory and its results emphasize the yin of sailboat motion, the air's driving and heeling forces that push and pull a sailboat to speed. In the theory, the yin forces are designated Left Hand side forces, and the yang forces as Right Hand side forces.

The general theory is presented in Chapter 3 and elaborated on in Chapter 5. Chapters 4 and 7 concern forms of representing resistance. Chapter 6 presents theorems and Lemmas for the sailboat based on the theory results. Example applications of the theory are presented in Chapters 8-12. Chapter 8 applies the theory to modern sailboats, both monohull and multihull.  Chapter 9 defines the limits of sailboat speed. Chapter 10 compares speeds predicted from the theory for selected high-speed sailboats to their actual recorded speeds and provides efficacy. Chapter 11 explores the sailing abilities of nonflapping stoneflies in view of the theory. Chapter 12 applies the theory to two vessels of antiquity. Chapter 12 also discusses a hypothetical ancient sailmaker, conversant with the general theory. The ancient sailmaker discusses the cut and placement of sails for the vessels of antiquity in terms of the general theory results. Proof that such a sailmaker could have been conversant with the general theory is provided. Illustrations are used throughout to communicate in figures what is also in words.

Chapter 2 gives definitions of elements basic to the theory. Chapter 3 is the heart of the general theory. There, the reduction of six equations of motion to three equations in order to represent the sailboat's motion is not new. However, *solving these equations by "the method of the free modulating function" is new*. It leads to the general theory and produces a primitive result called raw wind forces. This result is an enlightening single expression that incorporates righting moment characteristics of any vessel and represents the driving force per pound displacement for any sailing vessel. Some philosophers, general scientists, and mathematicians may find interesting the method of solving three simultaneous equations of motion by the definition and application of a "free modulating function."

Some of the Right Hand side forces in the three equations, which represent the responding resistance forces are used to modify the first primitive result of raw wind forces in Chapter 3 to available wind forces in Chapter 5. The entire Right Hand side forces provide the necessary balance forces to produce predicted equilibrium boat speeds in the example applications to real sailboats of Chapters 8, 9, 10, and 12. The reader will want to run a finger around the contours of sailboat speed possibilities that are illustrated for modern sailboats in Chapter 8.

The general theory is a flat surface theory. The source pair of true wind speed, *VTW*, and boat speed, *VB*, at a true wind angle, *ϴTW*, that generates an apparent wind speed, *VAW*, at an apparent wind angle, *ß*, is represented throughout as in Figure 1-1A. In other texts, *VAW* is generated as shown in Figure 1-1B by assuming a *-VB* wind acts on the sailboat that combines with *VTW* to produce *VAW*. The *VAW* of Figure 1-1B is the same as that in Figure 1-1A. However, the form of representation of Figure 1-1A that produces *VAW* is convenient for imagining all possibilities for the sailboat at all true wind angles. This is important since representing all the equilibrium speed possibilities for all sailing vessels on smooth waters is what the general theory is about.

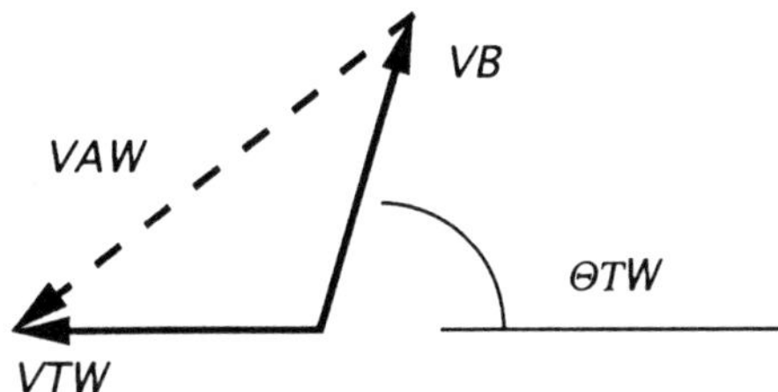


*A. Source Pair and Apparent Wind, VAW*

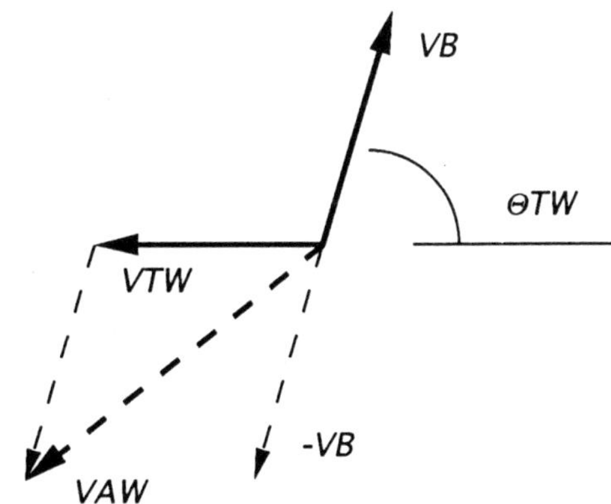


*B. Common Production of VAW*

Figure 1-1
Source Pair and *VAW* Representations

There is symmetry in the bird's-eye view of source pair representations as seen in the illustrations. As a result of this symmetry,
sailing the boat of the theory on one side of the wind is sufficient
to represent both sides of the wind. This means that the results
for $\theta TW$ from 0° to 180° for a starboard tack wind are sufficient
to represent the results for a port tack wind as well. A starboard
tack wind means the apparent wind, $VAW$, and the true wind
flow over the right side of the sailboat as a person onboard the
vessel faces the bow in the direction of motion, $VB$. (See Figure
1-2.)

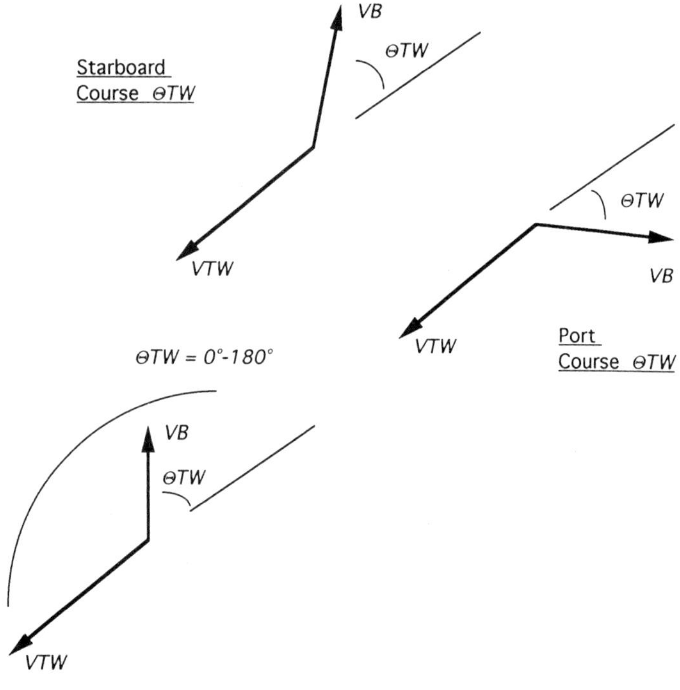


Figure 1-2
Symmetry of Flat Surface Representation

Some formulas are used in the representation of these concepts. All formulating quantities are considered positive at equilibrium speed for the starboard sailing half plane of symmetry. Thus boat speed, *VB*, true wind speed, *VTW*, true wind angle, $\Theta TW$, apparent wind speed, *VAW*, apparent wind angle, *ß*, drag coefficient for the sail-rig, $C_D$, lift coefficient for the sail rig, $C_L$, and leeway angle, $\lambda$, for the hull are all positive as in Figure 1-3.

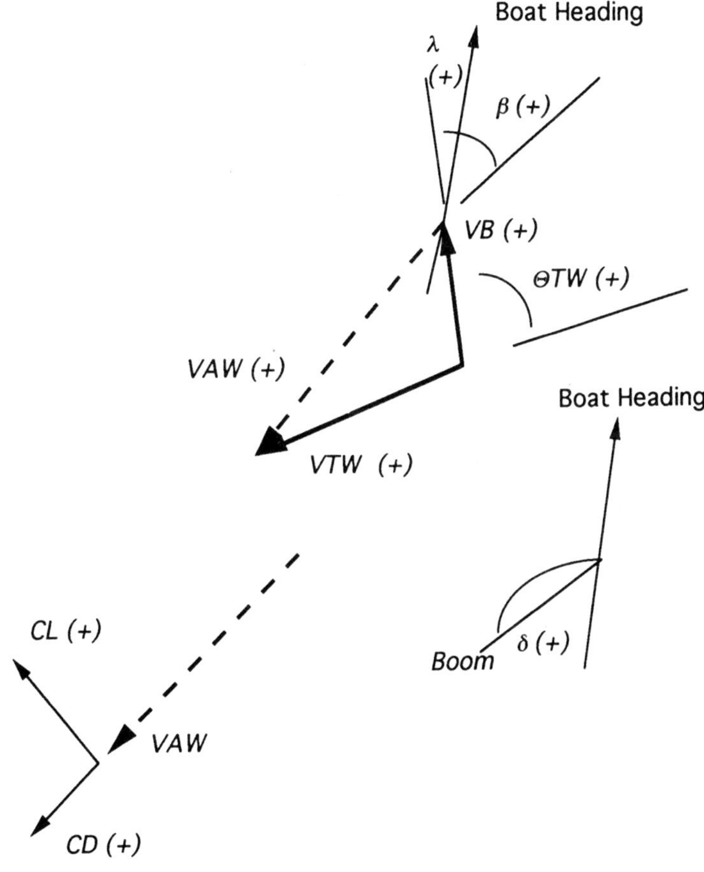


Figure 1-3
All Elemental Quantities Are Positive (+)

The limit speeds presented in Chapter 9 may explode some myths,
but their purpose is to demonstrate a dynamic of the general
theory. The defining of the limit speeds is a highlight application.
The limits found are compared with the limit speed predictions of
other authors.

The main body of the treatise is presented in Chapters 1-10. Chapters 11 and 12 are *zusatz* chapters. The results in Chapters 3 and 5
that incorporate righting moment in a single expression, represent
fundamental, new understandings for the sailboat. They show that
the character of the wind's forces for a sailboat in controlled
sailing is very important in determining the sailboat's speed on
smooth waters.

Following the concluding chapter (12), there are appendices that
include charts. The charts represent some driving force possibilities for the sailboat based on the general theory primitive result of
Chapter 3.  There is also  a glossary of terms used in the text.

Chapter 2 presents the definitions necessary for the general theory
presented in Chapter 3.  One consequence of the theory-primitive
is that sail area (S.A.) and displacement ($\Delta$) are not explicit in the
expression that represents the driving forces per pound displacement for all sailboats, but ratios of lengths and angles associated
with the sailboat's motion are explicit in that expression.

# Chapter 2 - Basic Concepts

This chapter presents tautologies, definitions, and assumptions essential to the theory of sailing. As used here, a tautology is something accepted without proof, like an axiom in mathematics. The definitions of sailing angles, the velocity triangle, Newtonian force balances, and drag and lift coefficients are all standard. Readers who are familiar with the sailing velocity triangle and force balances can skip this chapter. However, for many readers, the precise definition of the angle of attack on the sails, $\Omega$, which includes an apparent wind angle, $\beta$, a leeway angle, $\lambda$, and a sailtrim angle, $\delta$, may be new. As an overview, Figure 2-1 contains a bird's-eye (topview) of all the angles for an upright sailboat in steady motion velocity, $VB$, at a true wind course angle, $\ominus TW$, to the true wind speed, $VTW$. $VTW$ and $VB$ are condensed to single lines in a source pair of velocities that originate from a single point, $P$. In condensing the speed of the sailboat and the speed of the surrounding air to single lines, the following assumptions are made:

1.  The air mass above a smooth surface, $\Sigma$, of uniform density, $\rho_a$, is moving on a line of uniform velocity, $VTW$, relative to some unspecified reference point.

2.  $VB$ on $\Sigma$ generates a wind, $-VB$, also of uniform density, $\rho_a$.

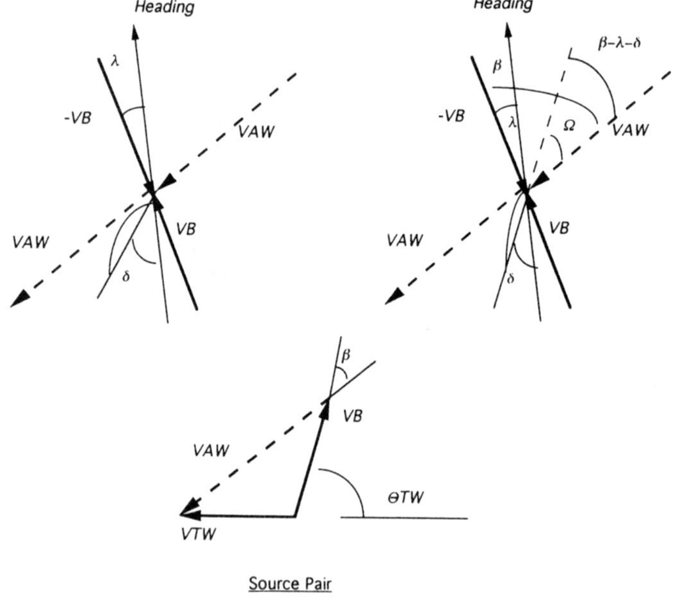


Figure 2 - 1
Bird's-Eye Overviews of Angles for a Sailboat in Motion
Projected to a Flat Surface Parallel to the Surface
on Which Motion Takes Place

Two independent tautologies occur for the sailboat sailing on a smooth flat surface. One concerns a velocity triangle, while the other concerns force balances rectangles (parallelograms). As is common practice, the two tautologies are connected via the square of the apparent wind velocity, $VAW$, generated from the source pair of $VB$ and $VTW$ and the velocity triangle defined. $VAW$ is generated by the motion of the sailboat's rig and sails moving at velocity, $VB$, relative to a fixed point on the earth through the air (which is moving at velocity $VTW$ relative to a fixed point on the earth). $VB$ and $VTW$ form two legs of the velocity triangle and generate $VAW$, the third leg.

Tautology I

The first tautology is that the wind can be condensed to a single line and that the wind generated by the boat's own speed can be condensed to a single line and that the condensed $-VB$ and $VTW$ lines can be added vectorially by way of a velocity triangle to produce a line of apparent wind, $VAW$, of density, $\rho_a$, in the vicinity of the sailboat that flows over and around membrane sails striking them at an apparent wind angle, ß, with an associated aerodynamic angle of attack, $\Omega$, to drive the sailboat forward at a course angle, $\Theta TW$, to the true wind, $VTW$, at boat speed, $VB$. (See Figure 2-2.)

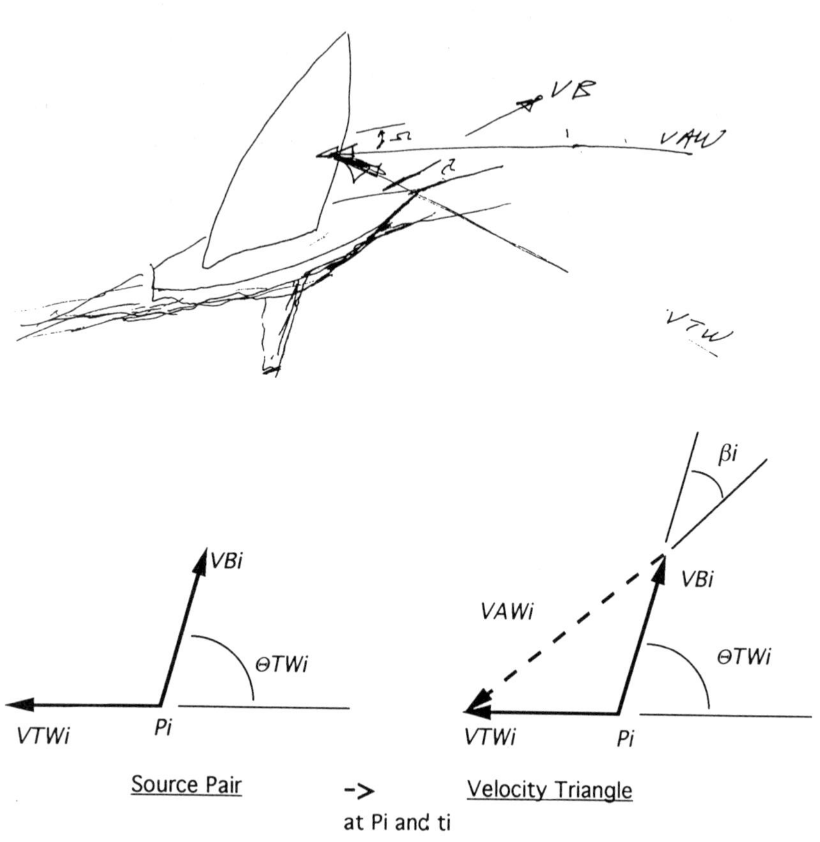



Figure 2-2
Sailboat and Overview of the Forming of the Velocity Triangle

Additional assumptions are made in order to represent the forces on the sails as mathematical quantities related to physical quantities—an idea attributed to Maxwell (1873)(D'Agostino, S. 1986, *Centaurus*, 29: 178-204). The additional assumptions are that the aerodynamic forces that drive and heel the sailboat object on $\Sigma_{smooth}$ at $P_i$ can be represented by a drag force, $D_i$, parallel to the direction of $VAW_i$ and a lift force, $L_i$, perpendicular to $VAW_i$ (see Figure 2-3) with lift generated by an angle of attack, $\Omega$, on the sails. The lift "vector" is in a plane parallel to $\Sigma$. The sail's chords are straight lines that connect the leading and trailing edges of the sail set. The angle of attack, $\Omega$, is the angle captured by the perpendicular projection of the line $VAW$ and the perpendicular projection of the line $VAW$ to the plane of the sail's chords.

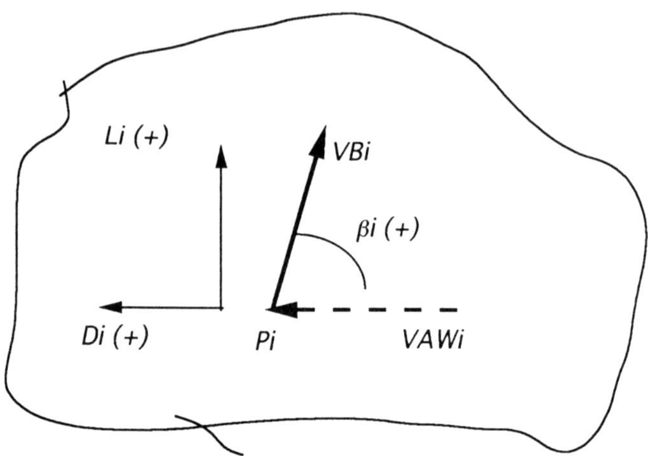


Plane Parallel to Σsmooth for a
Boat with No Angle of Heel

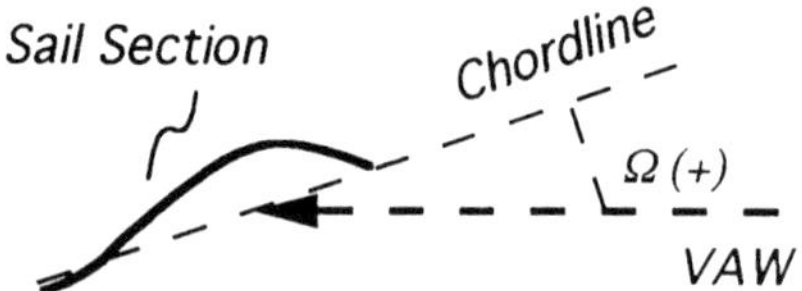


Figure 2-3
Top View of Drag and Lift on Sails
and VAW with Positive (+) Sign Defined

The drag and lift forces are represented by a triplet of numbers, $C_L$ or $C_{Di}$, $q_{ai}$, and $S.A._i$, where $C_{Di}$ is a drag coefficient, $q_{ai}$ is the kinetic energy density of the forward force-driving air mass defined as $1/2\, \rho_a\, VAW^2$ and $S.A._i$ is the projected plan form area of the rig-sails to the plane of the chords or a vertical plane through the centerline of the boat with the sails trimmed to the centerline and $C_{Li}$ is a lift coefficient.

thus,

$$D_i \;=\; C_{Di}\, q_{ai}\, S.A._i$$

and likewise

$$L_i \;=\; C_{Li}\, q_{ai}\, S.A._i$$

Experimetalists have found that $C_{Di}$ and $C_{Li}$ are related to the angle of attack, $\Omega$, and the line of $VAW$. (See Marchaj 1967, etc.) The $i$ subscript refers to the assumption that these quantities occur at the point $i$.

In Figure 2-4 the boat's heading is shown to differ from $VB$ by an angle, $\lambda$. The leeway angle, $\lambda$, modifies the angle of attack for sails trimmed to the centerline of the boat and no heel angle. With positive $\lambda$ at equilibrium speed, the angle of attack equals the apparent wind angle minus the leeway angle, or in symbol form $\Omega = \beta - \lambda$ ($\lambda$ is positive when the heading of the boat is towards the line of $VAW$). When $\lambda$ is zero, and the angle of heel is zero, and the sails are trimmed to the centerline of the boat so that $\delta$ is zero, then $\Omega = \beta$.

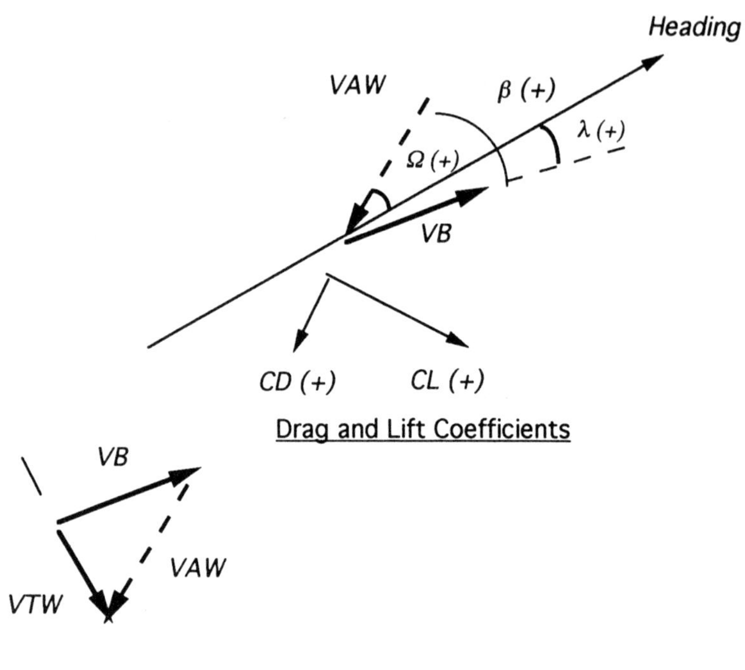



Figure 2-4
Drag and Lift Coefficients from VAW Action on the Sails
Trimmed to the Centerline of the Boat (Port Tack)

Tautology II

The second tautology is that the lift forces, $L_i$, and drag forces, $D_i$, generated by the moving air mass can be combined to form a driving force, $F_{adf}$, in the direction of steady motion velocity, $VB$, and another force, a sideways-pulling/heeling force, $F_{ahf}$, that is perpendicular to $VB$. These forces can be written mathematically in triplet form as the following:

$$F_{adf} = C_{Fi} \, q_{ai} \, S.A._i$$
$$F_{ahf} = C_{Hi} \, q_{ai} \, S.A._i$$

where

    $C_F$ = a driving force coefficient in the direction of motion at the point $i$

and

    $C_H$ = a heeling force coefficient perpendicular to the direction of motion at the point $i$

    $q_{ai}$ = kinetic energy density of the air flow $VAW$, $1/2 \, \rho_a VAW^2$

    $S.A._i$ = plan form sail area of the sail-rig

    $\rho_a$ = density of air

From here forward, the subscript $i$ will be dropped, but it is understood that all the symbols are associated with a point $i$ that moves on a flat surface. (See Figure 2-5.)

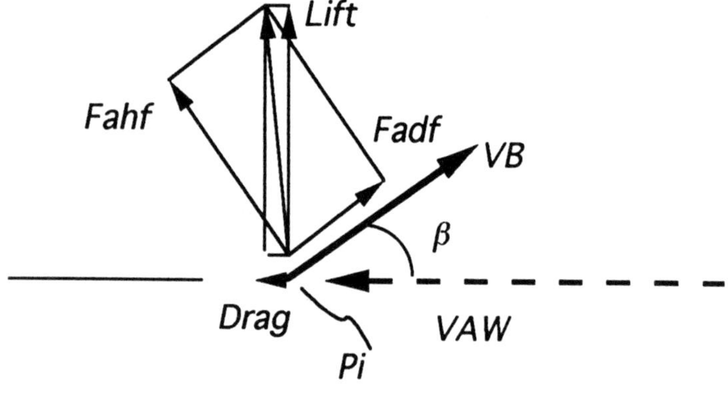


Figure 2-5
Driving and Heeling Forces Acting on the Sailboat

16

Resisting forces to the driving forces of the air are developed by flows of water by and about the boat's hulls or hull, and the boat's appendages, keels, and rudders. The water flows develop from the boat's forward motion, the water flowing relative to the boat in the direction -$VB$. The water flows, in turn, develop balancing forces to $F_{adf}$, opposite in direction to $F_{adf}$, called $F_{wrf}$. The balancing forces to the sideways-heeling force of the air, $F_{ahf}$, called $F_{whf}$, are opposite in direction to $F_{ahf}$. The assumption of these balancing forces leads to the basic equations of equilibrium motion when the boat is underway at a steady $VB$.

Throughout the text, the velocity triangle generates an apparent wind angle in the air, $ß$. The steady motion of the sailboat keel is associated with leeway angle of attack $\lambda$ with respect to the boat's heading (that is, the direction along the boat's centerline). This angle of attack, $\lambda$, for the water flow onto and about the fixed symmetric keel surfaces is what generates the balancing force, $F_{whf}$, for the fixed symmetrical keel.

Together with $\lambda$ and $ß$, two other overview angles describe the basic angles for sailboat motion in an upright mode: the already-mentioned angle of attack, $\Omega$, for $VAW$ on the sails, and a trim angle for the boom, $\delta$. The boom in some instances can be taken as a chord line for the sails and the angle, $\delta$, is in relation to the centerline of the boat. In sum, the angle of attack, $\Omega$, for the upright boat equals the apparent wind angle, $ß$ (generated by the sailboat's motion, and the true wind), minus the leeway angle, $\lambda$, minus the sail's angle of trim $\delta$, or $\Omega = ß - \lambda - \delta$. A summary of all these angles is repeated in Figure 2-6 along with forces generated on the sails.

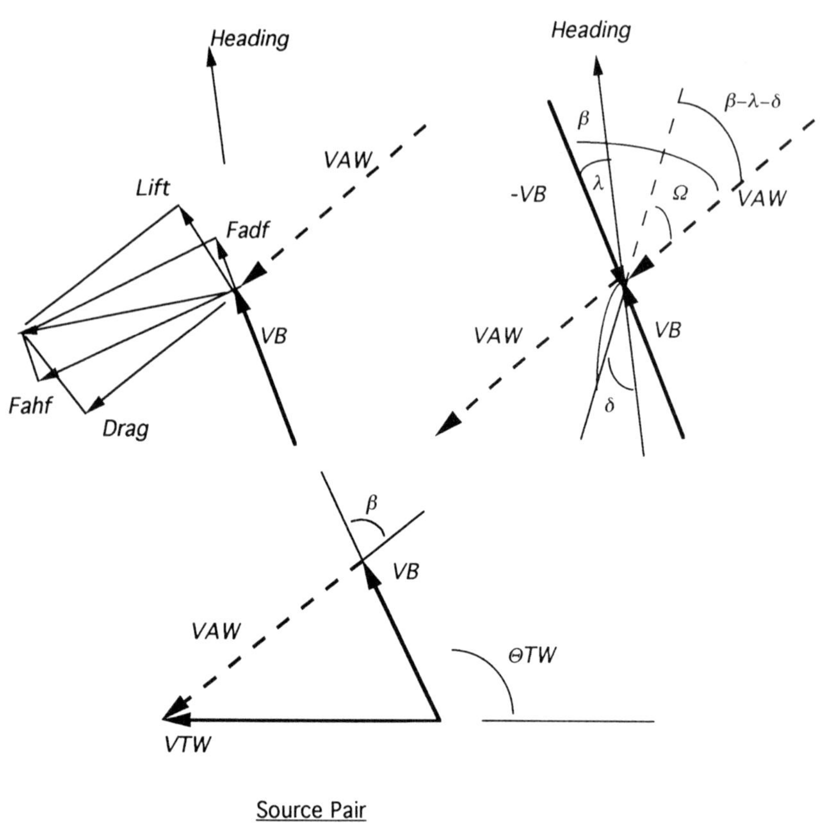



Figure 2-6
An Overview of Angles and Forces on the Sails for an
Upright Sailboat Projected to a Flat Surface
Parallel to the Surface on which Motion Takes Place
(Starboard Course Illustrated)

18

These angles, force balance definitions, assumptions, and tautologies are basic to the theory presented in the next chapter for the upright-sailing sailboat. It is not new that a point, $P_i$, can move according to a velocity triangle defined by a boat speed, $VB$, at an angle $\theta TW$ to $VTW$, generating an onboard $VAW$ and subject to force balances. However, the method used in the next chapter to solve the equations of motion is new. Furthermore, the primitive expressions produced from solving the equations that represent the sailboat are also new.

# Chapter 3 - The General Theory and a New Invariant

This chapter presents the general theory. Two new primitive expressions are produced from the theory's concepts. Those expressions are used to generate representational charts. Understanding the primitive results from the theory and the charts is the basis for making advances in the understanding of the sailboat's motion in nature. There is new matter of consequence to ponder and use in this chapter! Some concepts are conventional, some are not.  Six equations of motion are reduced to three. That is standard. The solving of these equations for equilibrium speed by the selective application of a free modulating function method is new. The results in this chapter are the core basis for subsequent applications of the theory in Chapters 8-12.

The theory is general, but its use in the example applications is restricted to sailboat objects whose condensed point representation, $Pi$, contains the righting moment of the sailboat it models in the form $B/H = 2arm_i/H$, where $B/H$ is a ratio of a catamaran type vesselbeam, $B$, to mast height, $H$. $Arm_i$ is the righting arm of the actual vessel modeled at whatever angle of heel. But, this is getting ahead of the general theory.

Equilibrium motion of the sailboat is defined by six force balance equations that correspond to six degrees of freedom; these are reduced to three force balance equations and three degrees of freedom.  The originating six degrees of freedom and six force balance equations are cast in a rectilinear coordinate system (a right-hand system of description) with three translation directions of velocity and three rotational directions. The translational velocities are forward, sideways, and heave (up and down). Each acts as a corresponding axis for rotational directions of motion. The rotational directions of motion are roll (rotation about the forward direction), pitch (rotation about the sideways direction), and yaw (rotation about the up-down heave direction). The complete set of equations and the reference system at $P_i$ are shown in Figure 3-1. The direction $x$ is parallel to or aligned with the steady motion velocity, $VB$, and the smooth flat surface, $\Sigma$. The force $F_{ax}$ is a force applied to the sailboat by the air in the direction $x$. $F_{wx}$ is the balance force in the water opposite to $F_{ax}$. $M_{ax}$ is a moment about the $x$ axis from forces of the air.

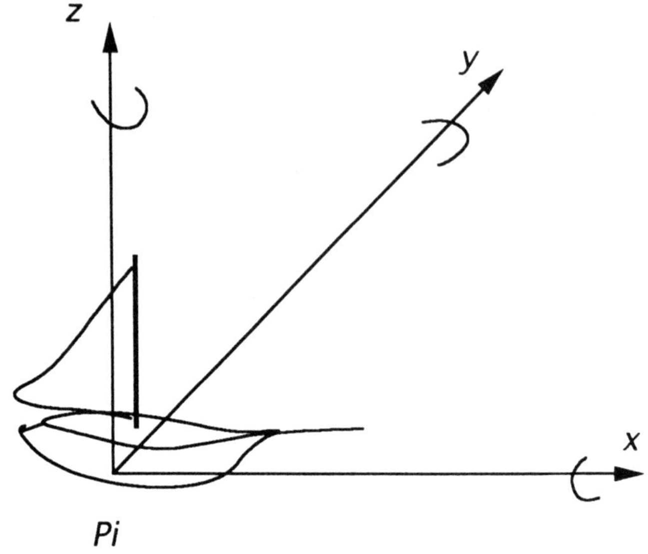


Translation Equations :
Fax  =  Fwx (forward)
Fay  =  Fwy (sideways)
Faz  =  Fwz (heave)
Rotation Equations :
Max)  =  Mwx) (roll)
May)  =  Mwy) (pitch)
Maz)  =  Mwz) (yaw)

Figure 3-1
The Reference System at $P_i$ with All Six Equations,
When the X Axis Is Parallel to or Aligned with VB

It is a complex problem to satisfy all six equations of motion simultaneously for a single vessel, even for iterative procedures on high-powered computers. It is common practice to reduce this set of six equations by various arguments to a set of three. In the general theory, the three equations of motion solved are those used extensively today to define the motion of a sailboat on smooth waters. They are for surge (forward speed), sway (leeway motion), and roll (angular heel about the forward motion axis). They apply for a steady forward speed, $VB$. Yaw angle, or leeway angle, $\lambda$, does appear in the sway equation. The yaw, pitch, and heave equations are of secondary importance in predicting the steady speed of sailboats on smooth waters (for example, see Milgram 1993, Van Ossen 1993). For a steady course with steady forward speed, steady sideways motion, and steady heeling motion, the sailboat problem is solved both generally and uniquely, noniteratively or with one iteration, as a sailboat moves from point 1 ($P_1$), to point 2 ($P_2$), from time 1 ($t_1$) to time 2 ($t_2$), at boat velocity1 ($VB_1$), where boat velocity at point 1 at time 1 equals boat velocity at point 2 at time 2, or $VB_1 = VB_2 = VB$, on a flat smooth surface, $\Sigma$.

In the general theory, the sailboat-vessel is condensed to a single point object with associated forces that make up the three basic force balances. The force balances below apply. Those forces on the Left Hand (LH) sides are attributed to the air and those on the Right Hand (RH) sides are attributed to the sea. The axis for $VB$ is aligned with the x-axis of the reference system. $F_{adf}$ is the driving forces of the air in the direction $VB$. $F_{wrf}$ is the resisting forces of the water opposite to the direction of $VB$. $F_{ahf}$ is the heeling/sideways forces from the air perpendicular to $VB$. $M_{ahf}$ is the heeling or overturning moment of the air's forces about the $VB$ axis. $M_{wrm}$ is the responding moment to the heeling moment.

|  | Air | Water |  |
| --- | --- | --- | --- |
| Translation in the direction of motion, $VB$ | $F_{adf}$ = | $F_{wrf}$ | (1) |
| Translation perpendicular to direction of motion, $VB$ | $F_{ahf}$ = | $F_{whf}$ | (2) |
| Rotation about axis of direction of motion, $VB$ | $M_{ahf}$ = | $M_{wrm}$ | (3) |

For the sailboats of the theory, *VB* is always aligned with the x-axis of Figure 3-1. The change in notation reflects that *VB* defines the x-axis and that all terms are considered positive (diophantine).

In order to solve these generally, Equation (1) is solved in two steps.

Step 1.  In Equation (1) the driving forces, Left Hand (LH) side and the resistance forces, Right Hand (RH) side, are both written as force per pound displacement weight. That is, $F_{adf}$ and $F_{wrf}$ are normalized with the displacement weight of the craft. Thus, Equation (1) is written with nondimensional forces as pound (lb) force per pound displacement weight, $\Delta$, of a craft moving at *VB*. For example, if the actual driving force $F_{adf}$ is 100 lbs and the vessel weighs 1000 lbs, $F_{adf}$ is 100 lbs/1000 lbs = 0.1 lb/lb = 0.1 (naturally, the RH side, *at equilibrium speed* will have a resistance per pound displacement of 0.1). $F_{adf}$ is written aerodynamically with an aerodynamic driving force coefficient, $C_F$, as

$$F_{adf} = C_F \, q_a \, S.A./\Delta \qquad (1A)$$

where

$C_F$ = a driving force coefficient in the direction of motion
$q_a$ = kinetic energy density of the air flow *VAW*, $1/2 \, \rho_a VAW^2$
S.A. = plan form sail area of the sail-rig
$\rho_a$ = density of air, and
$\Delta$ = displacement weight of the vessel

Step 2.  A free modulating function, $\eta$, is defined and applied by selective application only to the driving force side, the LH side, of Equation (1). And Equation (1) becomes

$$\eta F_{adf} = F_{wrf} \qquad (4)$$

Explicit Definition of the Free Modulating Function

For the solution of this set of equations, the modulating function
of Equation (4) is defined *as the ratio of righting moment available to the righting moment required* at each speed, VB, and as a
free function.

$$\eta = \frac{\text{Righting Moment Available}}{\text{Righting Moment Required}} \quad \begin{matrix} < & 1 \\ = & 1 \\ > & 1 \end{matrix}$$

The righting moment required is the righting moment required of
the wind. The righting moment available is the righting moment
available from the sailboat and all related sources to counter the
righting moment required of the air. If interpreted in the currently
conventional way for a sailboat, $\eta = 1$, the modulating function
is just Equation (3) written differently. In this work $\eta$ begins
"free," that is, less than 1, or equal to 1, or greater than 1, and it
is applied to the LH side of Equation (1) only. Later on, for a
specific boat with a specific resistance curve at an equilibrium
speed, it is made to equal 1, or interpreted as 1 for that speed
and that vessel. With $\eta = 1$ at $VB_{equilibrium}$, it is possible to identify
specific physical characteristics about a vessel after the problem is
solved. Again, in step 2, Equation (1) becomes Equation (4) *where
the LH side of (1) is modified by a free modulating function.*

Equation (4) is a "nondimensional force balance" in a gravity
system, where g acceleration on $\Sigma$ is a constant and the sailboat
mass is a constant, so weight, $(W_i)$, equals mass $(m_i)$ times accelerations of gravity $g_i$ and $W_i = \Delta_i$. (This is a detail that becomes
important for later developments of the theory.) With $\eta$ appearing
only on the driving side of the equation for forward translational
motion, the equations are now as follows:

Translation in direction of motion, VB $\quad \eta\, F_{adf} = F_{wrf}$ (4)
Translation perpendicular to
direction of motion $\quad\quad\quad\quad\quad\quad F_{ahf} = F_{whf}$ (2)
Rotation about axis
in direction of motion, VB $\quad\quad\quad\quad M_{ahf} = M_{wrm}$ (3)

The method of the selective application of a free modulating
function has produced a new set of equations to be solved in
equilibrium boat speed for smooth water conditions for any
sailboat.  While Equations (2) and (3) remain the same, Equation
(1) has become Equation (4) and is at the focus of the process for
solving the new set of all three equations for all the possibilities
for a sailboat on smooth waters.

What Does $\eta\, F_{adf}$ Look Like?

Recall that $F_{adf} = C_F\, q_a\, S.A./\Delta$ and the definition of $\eta$ is,

$$\eta \;=\; \frac{\text{Righting Moment Available}}{\text{Righting Moment Required}} \quad \begin{array}{ll} < & 1 \\ = & 1 \\ > & 1 \end{array}$$

In order to explore $\eta$ it is necessary to give more definition to
Righting Moment Available and Righting Moment Required for
the sailboat. Righting Moment Available is general. It is from any
and all hydrodynamic, static, and mechanical sources built into
the boat's design or the actual boat and from placement of live
ballast crew athwartship, or movement of dead ballast bags
(sometimes called sand bagging), or a combination of all sources.
Although it may be generated by more than one factor, it is
defined in the form of displacement weight, $\Delta$, times an arbitrary
arm, $arm_i$, for each speed or sailing condition, thus

$$\text{Righting Moment Available} = \Delta\, arm_i$$

Righting Moment Required is assumed to develop from the action
of the apparent wind on the sail-rig. It is an action that produces
aerodynamic heeling forces on the rig to go with the driving
forces. It is defined as aerodynamic heeling force, $F_{ahf}$, times a
heeling arm, $\mu H$, where $H$ is the mast height above deck in the
air, and $\mu$ is a fraction. In symbol form,

$$\begin{aligned}\text{Righting Moment Required} &= F_{ahf}\, \mu H \\ &= C_H q_a\, S.A.\, \mu H\end{aligned}$$

where

$C_H$ = a heeling force coefficient perpendicular to the direction of
    motion
$q_{ai}$ = kinetic energy density of the air flow $VAW$, $1/2\, \rho_a VAW^2$
$S.A._i$ = plan form sail area of the sail-rig
$\rho_a$ = density of air

So the modulating function begins to take form. It is the ratio, at each possible speed, $VB$, of an arbitrary righting arm times the vessel displacement divided by the heeling moment generated by wind forces acting on the sails (the same wind simultaneously generates forces to drive the boat forward). In symbol form,

$$\eta = \frac{\Delta\, arm_i}{C_H\, q_a\, S.A.\, \mu H} \quad \begin{array}{l} < \ 1 \\ = \ 1 \\ > \ 1 \end{array}$$

When $\eta$ is less than 1, there is rolling, possibly leading to capsize; when $\eta$ is equal to 1 there is a steady angle of heel; and when $\eta$ is greater than 1, there may be rolling in the opposite direction. By adding more form to $\eta$, the LH side of Equation (4) on the substitution for $F_{adf}$ takes on a general vessel-related form with

$$\eta\, F_{adf} = \frac{\Delta\, arm_i}{C_H\, q_a\, S.A.\, \mu H} \quad C_F q_a\, (S.A./\Delta) \quad *$$

which produces the first primitive result for this application of $\eta$ as

$$\eta\, F_{adf} = (arm_i/H)\, (C_F\, /C_H)\, (1/\mu) \qquad (5) \ **$$

Thus far no specific craft has been specified except that

1. It must be one that has a mast to mount sails on with mast height, $H$, and wind-heeling arm, $\mu H$.
2. The velocity and force balance tautologies apply, and

3.  There are heeling moments from the air and righting
    moments from the action of the water underway, plus me-
    chanical, and ballast possibilities.

The sailboat can still be thought of as in Figure 3-1, with a few
physical characteristics added. The new physical characteristics
are a heeling arm, $\mu H$, a righting arm of $arm_i$, a driving force
coefficient, $C_F$, and a heeling coefficient, $C_H$. This is a stick boat
moving as shown in Figure 3-2. It contains these physical factors
even though they are not shown in the figure. The stick boat has
a mast height, $H$, and freeboard height, $zf$, and keel depth, $d$.
Conceptually, the stick boat of Figure 3-2 just precedes the complete condensing of a sailboat to a single point that carries physical attributes of the sailboat.

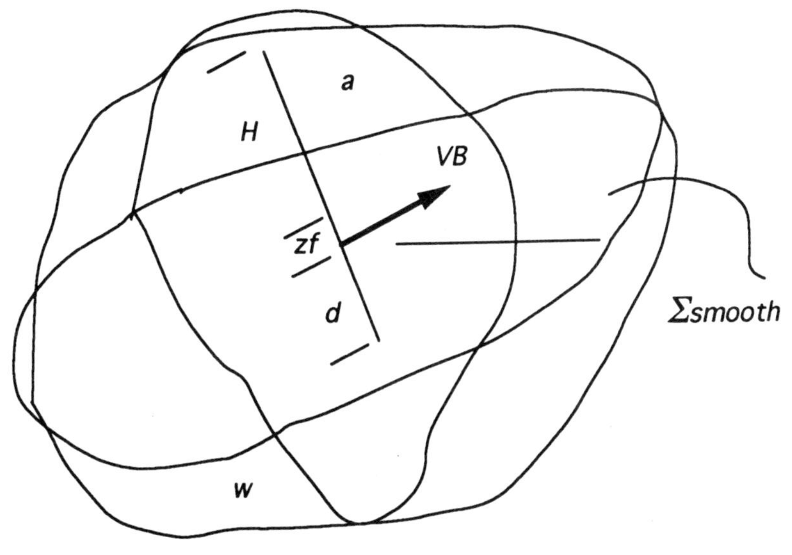


*H = Mast Height*
*zf = Freeboard*
*d = draft*

Figure 3-2
Stick Boat Moving on Surface Σ with Mast Height, *H*,
and Freeboard Height, *zf*, and Keel Depth, *d*

The primitive result in Equation (5) is maximized to make it interpretable for all sailboats. To maximize (5), it is applied to a specific vessel of known $arm_i$ at $\Theta_{Hi} = \Theta_{Hmax}$, where $\Theta_{Hi}$ is the angle of heel, and $\Theta_{Hmax}$ is the maximum angle of heel. Equation (5) is first applied to a catamaran of beam, $B$, at hull-afly speed with all crew weight in the center cockpit. It has a maximum righting arm of $1/2\ B$ and $W = \Delta$ as illustrated in Figure 3-3.

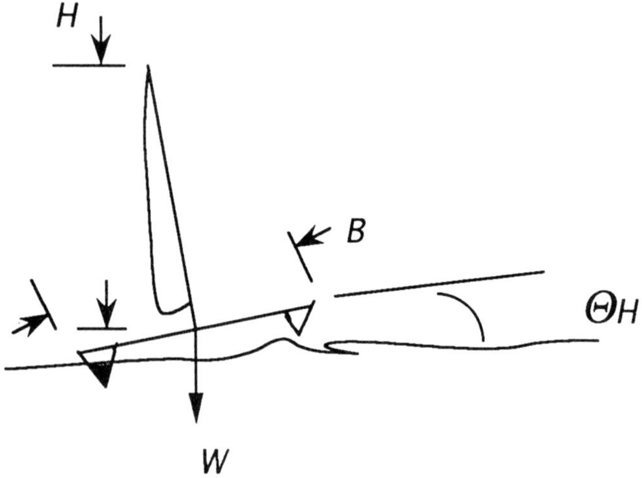


$H$ = Mast Height
$B$ = Catamaran Beam
$W$ = Weight
$\Theta H$ = Angle of Heel

Figure 3-3
Catamaran at Hull-Afly Speed, $W = \Delta$

The catamaran in Figure 3-3 is hull-afly from astern. The weather hull just skims the surface. The craft is heeled by forces from the apparent wind while moving at speed, $VB$. Hull-afly provides a maximum heeling moment. For the cat at hull-afly, $arm = 1/2\ B \cos \Theta_H$, which is approximately equal to $1/2\ B/H$ for $\Theta_H$ less than $10°$, the assumed hull-afly heeling angle for the catamaran. ($Cos 10° = .9848$, which is nearly 1.0. So 1.0 is used as the value for $\cos \Theta_H$). Equation (5) becomes Equation (6).

$$((1/2B)/H)\ (C_F/C_H)\ (1/\mu) = $$
$$(B/H)\ (C_F/C_H)\ (1/2\mu) \qquad\qquad (6) \ ***$$

Thus the driving force of the catamaran at hull-afly is defined by three ratios, the ratio of beam to mast height, the ratio of driving force coefficient to heeling force coefficient, and the ratio of 1 to twice the fraction $\mu$.

This second primitive, Equation (6)***, represents the driving force per pound displacement for the sailboat. While it is wrought for a catamaran at hull-afly, it applies for any sailboat where a $B/H = 2\ arm/H$ exists and $C_F$ and $C_H$ can be defined clearly. It is quite general in its representation powers, and Equation (4) becomes Equation (7)

$$\text{air} \qquad\qquad\qquad \text{water}$$
$$(B/H)\ (C_F/C_H)\ (1/2\mu) = F_{wrf} \qquad\qquad (7)$$

From here forward, the LH side of Equation (7) is considered to apply to a sailboat sailing upright. Even so, the theory still applies to sailboats that heel and produce a righting arm from the heeling. The righting characteristics are absorbed into the moving point. (The affects of heeling are addressed in Chapter 8 for applications to real sailboats.) The boat that sails on the LH side of Equation (7) is upright with righting arms from heeling attached. The boat that sails on subsequent charts produced to demonstrate the theory is also upright. These are boats of the imagination with consequences. They carry the righting arm of the monohull or catamaran or trimaran modeled in reality moving with point $P_i$. Inside every monohull, or any type sailing vessel of the theory, there is a catamaran, hull-afly, sailing with a corresponding-equivalent $B/H$ ratio, $B/H_{equivalent}$. Hereafter, $(B/H)$ is understood to be the same as $(B/H)_{equivalent}$.

Upright or heeled, $C_F$ and $C_H$ can be written as functions of an apparent wind angle, ß. The associated lift and drag coefficients for the rig are functions of $\Omega$. The associated lift and drag coefficients for the rig can also be written as functions of ß. As all the angles in Chapter 2 show, the aerodynamic angle $\Omega$ is equal to the apparent wind angle ß minus the leeway angle, $\lambda$, minus the sailtrim angle, $\delta$: $\Omega = ß - \lambda - \delta$. When $C_L$ and $C_D$ for the upright boat's sail-rig are written first as functions of the aerodynamic angle $\Omega$, then, under certain conditions, they can become functions of just the apparent wind angle, ß.

When $C_F$ and $C_H$ and $B/H$ are all in a force system aligned with $VB$, then for the upright boat,

$$\Omega = ß - \lambda - \delta$$

and

$$C_F = C_L(\Omega) \, [sin\ ß - (C_D/C_L)(\Omega)\ cos\ ß]$$
$$C_H = C_L(\Omega) \, [cos\ ß + (C_D/C_L)(\Omega)\ sin\ ß]$$

When the trim angle, $\delta$, is zero, and the boom is trimmed to the boat's centerline, $\Omega$ equals $ß - \lambda$ and

$$C_F = C_L\ (ß - \lambda)\ [sin\ ((ß)) - (C_D/C_L)\ (ß - \lambda)\ cos\ ((ß))]$$
$$C_H = C_L\ (ß - \lambda)\ [cos\ ((ß)) + (C_D/C_L)\ (ß - \lambda)\ sin\ ((ß))]$$

When $\lambda$ is small ($< 2°$) and $\delta$ is equal to 0, then $\Omega$ is approximately equal to ß and

$$C_F = C_L\ (ß)\ [sin\ ß - (C_D/C_L)\ (ß)\ cos\ ß]$$
$$C_H = C_L\ (ß)\ [cos\ ß + (C_D/C_L)\ (ß)\ sin\ ß]$$

Sets of $C_D/C_L$, $C_L$, or $C_D$, $C_L$ for a sailboat can be related to an $\Omega$ base set, or a ß base set, or a combination of both sets. The drag and lift coefficients for $\Omega$ base and ß base representations only become the same when $\Omega$ equals ß. The angle ß is emphasized because it can be readily found from the velocity triangle for every given source pair of $VTW$ and $VB$ and for every $\ominus TW$. On the sailboat with an actual sail-rig combination, $C_D$ is a function of $\beta$ and $C_L$ is a function of $\Omega$. This treatise assumes that for a range of $\beta$, $C_D/C_L$ can be identified or assumed for the sail-rig combination that drives the sailboat, and that the set of $C_D/C_L$ can be related to a set of $\Omega$ or a set of $\beta$ or a combination set of both. Also, the theory assumes that sail-rig is trimmed such that it develops some lift and some drag at each boat speed $VB$. So its application is for $\ominus TW$ from $0°$ to just less than $180°$ (about $170°$). It is the set $C_D/C_L$ as a function of $\beta$ that is emphasized in general theory results.

$B/H$ in Equation (6) may be a function of $\lambda$ as the boat acquires righting moment by rotating about the $VB$ axis. Righting moment may vary with $\lambda$. In the instant of a catamaran at hull-afly, the righting arm becomes $1/2\ B\ \cos\lambda$, which is approximately $1/2\ B$ for $\lambda < 10°$. In the rest of this treatise $B/H$ is $B/H$ in general. For whatever vessel is being considered, monohull or multihull, $2arm/H$ is formed for the vessel and defined as $B/H$ equivalent for the theory. $B/H$ is used as a general-descriptive variable because it is easy to imagine a catamaran with hulls that move closer together or further apart in motion. Just such an imagined catamaran is the basis for the development of the second primitive, Equation (6)***.

The overall solution method uses the following procedure. Equation (7) is solved first, in a LH side = RH side equation for $VB_{equilibrium}$ before Equations (2) and (3) are made to balance. In other words, when given a true wind angle, $\ominus TW$, and true wind speed, $VTW$ and $B/H$ and $\lambda$ and $\delta$, and a resistance curve, then, an equilibrium $VB$ from Equation (7) is found, and the equilibrium speed found is assumed to act for Equations (2) and (3). The solution speed $VB$ (from the intersect of driving forces per pound displacement for a given $VTW$ and a resistance curve per pound displacement), provides $\beta$, $VB$, and $VAW$. (3) is met automatically, providing that $C_L$ S.A. and $B/H$ and $1/2\mu$ are achievable by the vessel, then (2) is solved for the necessary keel variables of keel area and lift slope to make it so. The solution method begins with an assumed or defined $B/H$ whether for a monohull or a multihull. The philosophy of solution is that inside every monohull or any sailing craft there is an equivalent sailing catamaran, and the craft sails at an equivalent *B/H* for use in the Equation (6)*** for the vessel's driving force per pound displacement. For a catamaran, *B/H* may be less than the vessel's maximum *B/H* capability.

To make it possible to find the initial solution that leads to an overall solution of all three equations, the LH side of (7) is given further explicit form by direct substitution for $C_F$ and $C_H$ so that

$$(B/H) \, (C_F / C_H) \, (1/2\mu) =$$

$$(B/H) \; \frac{[\sin(\beta) - (C_D/C_L)(\Omega)\cos(\beta)]}{[\cos(\beta) + (C_D/C_L)(\Omega)\sin(\beta)]} \; (1/2\mu) \qquad (8) \; ****$$

This expression represents the driving force per pound displacement of upright sailboats and includes righting moment characteristics of the vessel. It is a new mathematical-physical invariant to represent the sailboat object of nature.

In the primitive Equation (8)****, the drag-to-lift ratio for the sails, $(C_D/C_L)$ can be a function of $\Omega = (\beta - \lambda - \delta)$, or it can be a function of $\beta$ with $\lambda$ and $\delta$ assumed to make $(C_D/C_L)$ true.

Bounds for $C_L$ and $C_D/C_L$, are known or can be produced from empirical tests for a range of possible $\Omega$, $\beta$ and $\lambda$ and $\delta$. For example, a bound for one type of sail may be $C_L < 1.4$ for $C_D/C_L = 0.15$, when $5° < \beta < 24°$.

When Equation (8) is interpreted in the form of making (*B/H*) a function of the apparent wind angle, $\beta$, boat speed, *VB*, and the righting characteristics assumed, and also $C_D/C_L$ is a function of $\beta$ and $\mu$ is a function of the type of keel and sails assumed, then it is true for all boats generally. When these are known specifically, it is true for a specific boat. The primitive of Equation (8) is thus general or specific.  It is a primitive because it is a root expression, a generating function that represents the sailboat.

Example Charts

Another possible interpretation is that $B/H$ and $\mu$ are fixed values for a class of sailboats, and $C_D/C_L$ is set for a range of $\beta$. Such an interpretation can be used to define charts for these classes of sailboats. Such charts from Equation (8) are called raw wind force (RAWF) charts. For example, if $B/H$ is defined as 0.8 and the range of $\beta$ is, $22° > \beta > 0°$, with $C_D/C_L = 0.15$, then charted values of Equation (8) versus boat speed represent the driving force for current blue water high-speed sailing vessels sailing at their maximum hull-afly $B/H$. Example charts with these values for $B/H$ and $C_D/C_L$ are shown in Figures 3-5, 3-6, 3-7, and 3-8. In the example charts, $\lambda$ and $\delta$ and the sail-rig are such that $C_D/C_L$ is achieved at each $VB$. The Raw Wind Forces, RAWFs, of Equation (8) are plotted versus $VB$ in these figures for course heading possibilities of $\ominus TW = 45°$, $\ominus TW = 90°$, $\ominus TW = 135°$, and $\ominus TW = 165°$. In each of these charts a boat is sailing at the given true wind angle and true wind speed, and at boat speeds that vary between 0 and 100 knots. Cusps occur for $\ominus TW = 135°$ and $\ominus TW = 165°$. These cusps are near $VB$ that corresponds to $\beta = 90°$, where $C_F/C_H -> 1 \div (C_D/C_L)$ and

$$RAWF -> (B/H) \times \frac{1}{C_D/C_L} \times \frac{1}{2\mu} \ .$$

The corresponding source pairs of $VB$ and $VTW$ for these charts are shown in the Figure 3-4.

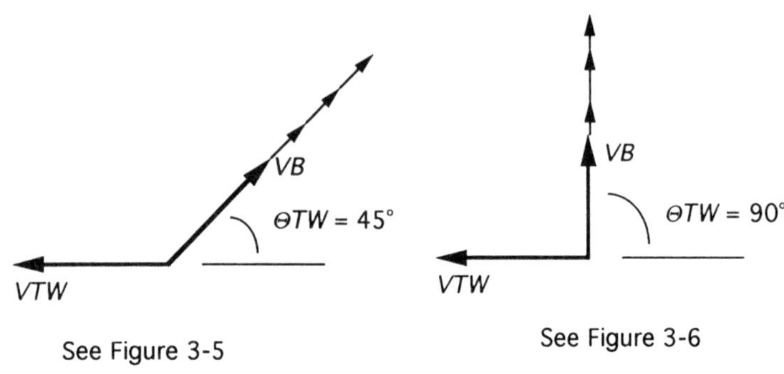


See Figure 3-5

See Figure 3-6

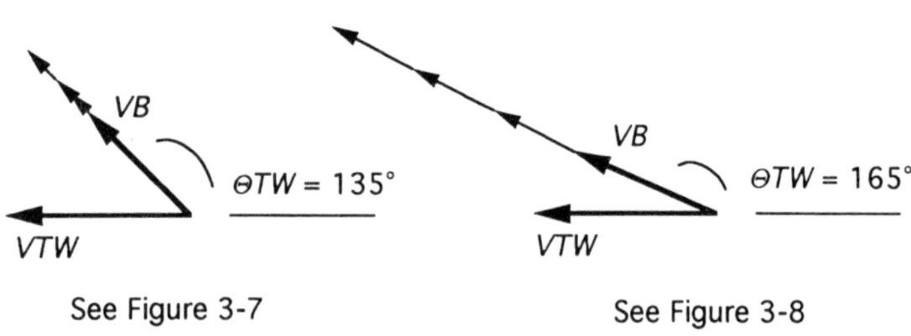


See Figure 3-7

See Figure 3-8

Figure 3-4
The Sailing Course Angles for Figures 3-5, 3-6, 3-7, and 3-8

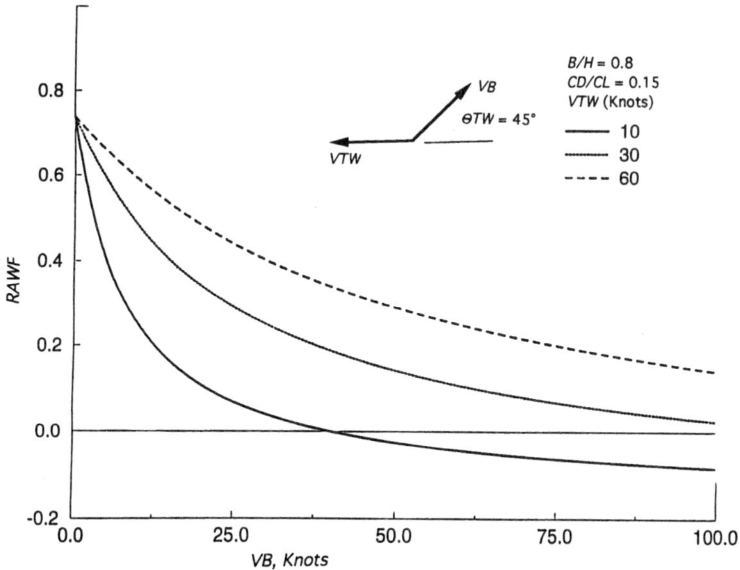


Figure 3-5
Raw Wind Forces, Three Wind Speeds,
and One True Wind Angle of 45°

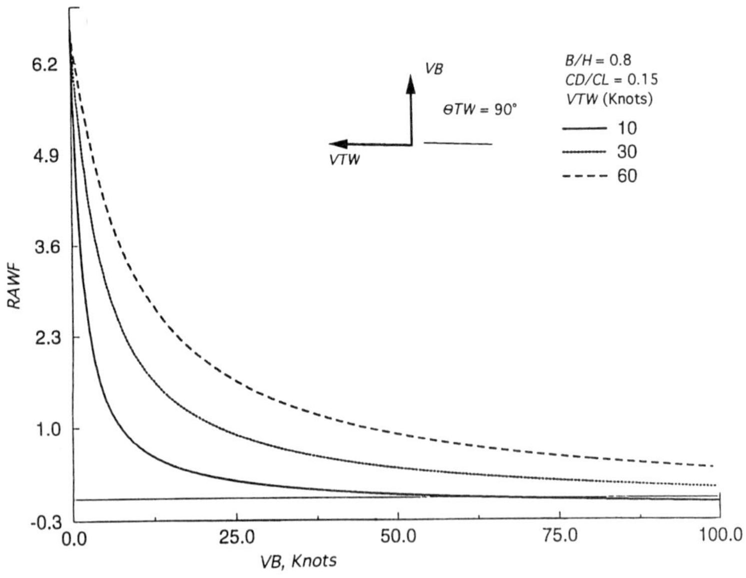


Figure 3-6
Raw Wind Forces, Three Wind Speeds,
One True Wind Angle of 90°

38

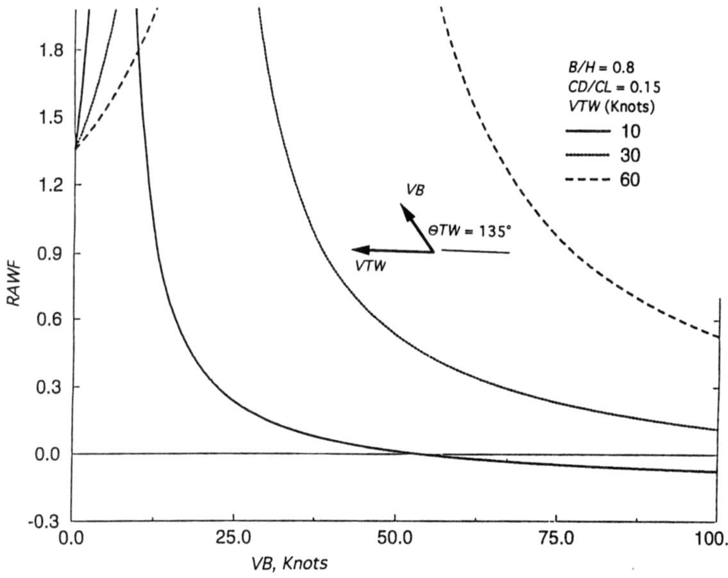



Figure 3-7
Raw Wind Forces, Three Wind Speeds,
One True Wind Angle of 135°

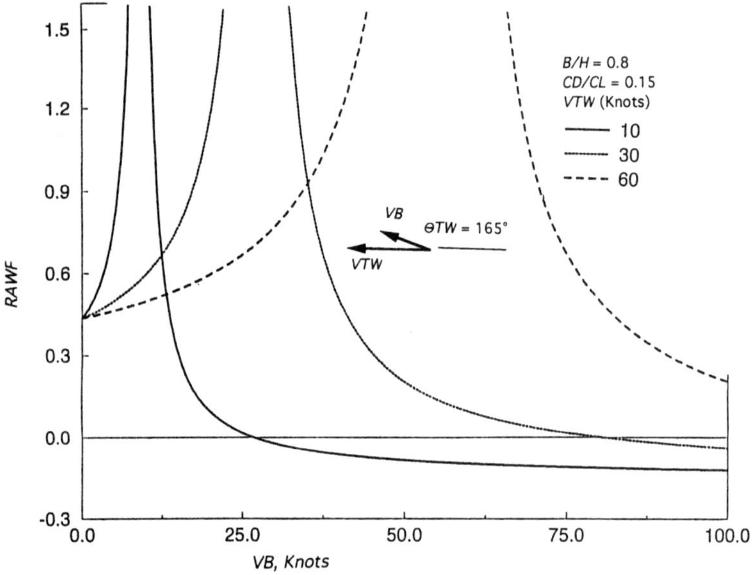



Figure 3-8
Raw Wind Forces, Three Wind Speeds,
One True Wind Angle of 165°

These initial charts represent driving force possibilities at each *VB* for a vessel at each *VB*, able to sustain or achieve, the prescribed *B/H* equivalent, and $C_F/C_H$ of efficiency $C_D/C_L$ and *(1/2μ)*. New things wrought from the theory are primitives of Equations (5)**, (6)*** and (8)****. *These are generating functions that include righting moment and generate driving force possibilities for the sailboat sailing at speed VB, steady true course angle, ⊖TW, with corresponding ß and λ, and with $C_D/C_L$ for the rig and B/H for the vessel.* Driving forces per pound displacement weight for four points of sail (45°, 90°,135°, and 165°) are summarized on one chart for 20 knots of true wind in Figure 3-9.

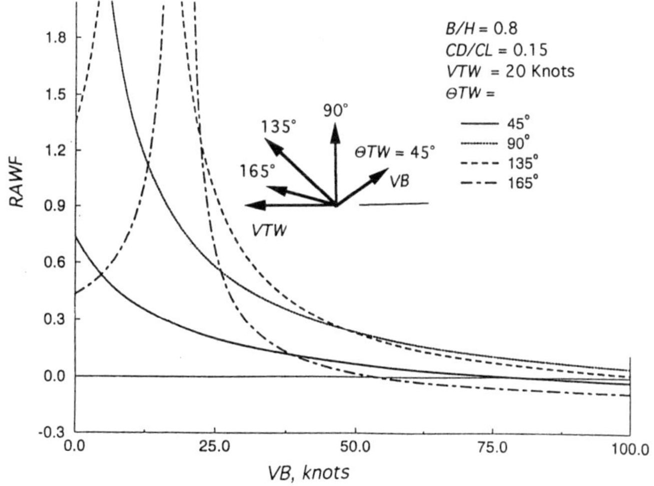


Figure 3-9
Raw Wind Forces, Four True Wind Angle Courses,
and One True Wind Speed of 20 Knots

In Figure 3-9, a $B/H = 0.8$ may not be achievable on every point of sail for a specific vessel. Also achievable $B/H$ may be a fraction of the chart value and vary with specific course and speed for a specific vessel.

In sum, when using the charts for speed predictions, $VB_{equilibrium}$ speed is found by adding a resistance curve to the charts herein, $\lambda$ can then be found/estimated from Equation (2) after $C_L$ $S.A./\Delta$ is found, or selected by use of Equation (3) with the known $B/H$ and $VB$ and $\beta$. In Chapter 5, RAWF is modified to Available Wind Force (AWF), but the method of solution of the equations of motion with AWF remains similar to that just described for RAWF. $VB_{equilibrium}$ is found first, then $C_L$ $S.A./\Delta$, then finally $\lambda$.

These theory results have consequences in furthering the understanding of the sailboat. Inspection of the figures for Raw Wind Forces versus boat speed makes it clear that *for a steady course, the faster a sailboat sails, the less driving force per pound displacement there is to drive it faster still.*

Further inspection of the figures makes it clear that *drawing almost any resistance curve for a specific sailboat through the charts will produce a predicted equilibrium boat speed for that vessel.* This makes the theory results general and is important for applications of the theory.

With use, the power and the usefulness of the charts is made clearer, first by the theorems of Chapter 6, then by the application examples in the Chapters 8-12. In Chapter 8 boat speeds for specific sailboats are predicted. The primitive, (6)***, makes it possible to define, in Chapter 9, the exciting limits of sailboat speeds for smooth waters and steady course.

A new method of solution for the equations of motion, the method of the free modulating function, has wrought primitive generating functions and charts for the forces that drive the sailboat; these are called Raw Wind Force (RAWF) charts. The next chapter focuses on the other sides of nature's balanced coins for the sailboat, the Right Hand sides of the equations for the sailboat in motion, the resistance sides, and righting moment side. They are the RH side pieces to the puzzle and compliment the LH driving force representations from the general theory for point $P_i$ sailing on a flat surface $\Sigma$ with raw wind force driving capabilities of the RAWF charts generated by the primitives of (5)**, (6)*** or (8)****, or with available wind force driving capabilities of the AWF charts of Chapter 5. See Figure 3-10.

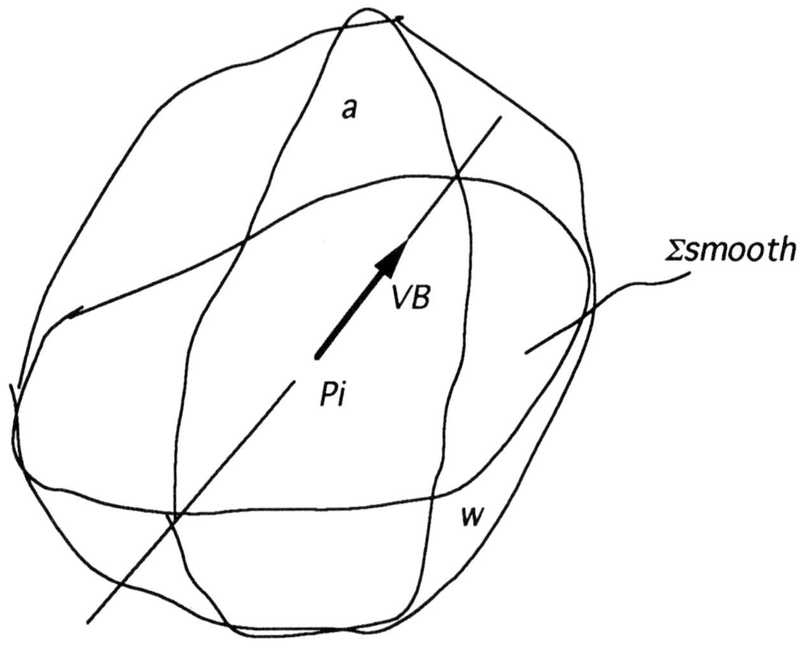


Figure 3-10
Sailboat of the General Theory Reduced to a Point, $P_i$,
Sailing on $\Sigma_{smooth/flat}$ with Air, a, Above and Water, w,
Below and with the Driving Force Capabilities
of the RAWF Charts

The method of the free modulating function applied to the equations of motion brought a new primitive expression for the driving force per pound displacement for the sailboat that includes righting moment characteristics for all sailing vessels. The primitive expression for driving force per pound displacement of Equation (6), together with the conventional expression for driving force per pound displacement of Equation (1A) provide a complete basis for the understanding of the sailboat.

$$F_{adf} = C_F \, q_a \, S.A./\Delta \qquad\qquad (1A)$$

$$F_{adf} = (B/H) \, (C_F \, /C_H) \, (1/2\mu) \qquad (6) \; {*}{*}{*}$$

The time to use $(B/H)$ $(C_F /C_H)$ $(1/2\mu)$ from the general theory or the conventional representation, $C_F \, q_a \, S.A./\Delta$, for driving forces per pound displacement depends on righting moment required. Righting moment required is reflected in the absolute value of the heeling/sideways coefficient of the sails, $|C_H|$, which depends on the apparent wind angle, ß, achievable by the vessel in each source pair and $(C_D/C_L)$. The apparent wind angle is governed in turn by the speed attainable at each true wind course, $\ominus TW$, possible in the source pair. Whenever the apparent wind angle is less than 90°, then, it is possible for the righting moment required by the modulating function to be zero. The equivalent statement is the $|C_H|$ -> 0 (-> means "goes to") at some $VB$ for $\ominus TW > 90°$. It occurs at some speeds, true wind courses and $(C_D/C_L)$ ratios. This can readily be seen by inspection of Figures 3-11 and 3-12.

In Figure 3-11 the true wind angle of the source pair depicted is 135°. Drag-to-lift ratios, $(C_D/C_L)$, are marked with straight edge and compass for example boat speeds where the apparent wind angle, ß, is greater than 90°, equal to 90° and less than 90°. For ß > 90°, the central example of $(C_D/C_L)$ is one where $|C_H|$ -> 0 and a cusp is formed in $RAWF$ representations of driving force per pound displacement for vessel sailing. See Figures 3-7 and 3-8. At speeds where a cusp is formed in $RAWF(|C_H|$ -> 0) it is better to use the conventional Equation (1A) for all speeds where ß is greater then 90°. At speeds where ß is less than 90°, Equation (6) *RAWF* representations are much preferred for driving force per pound displacement representations.

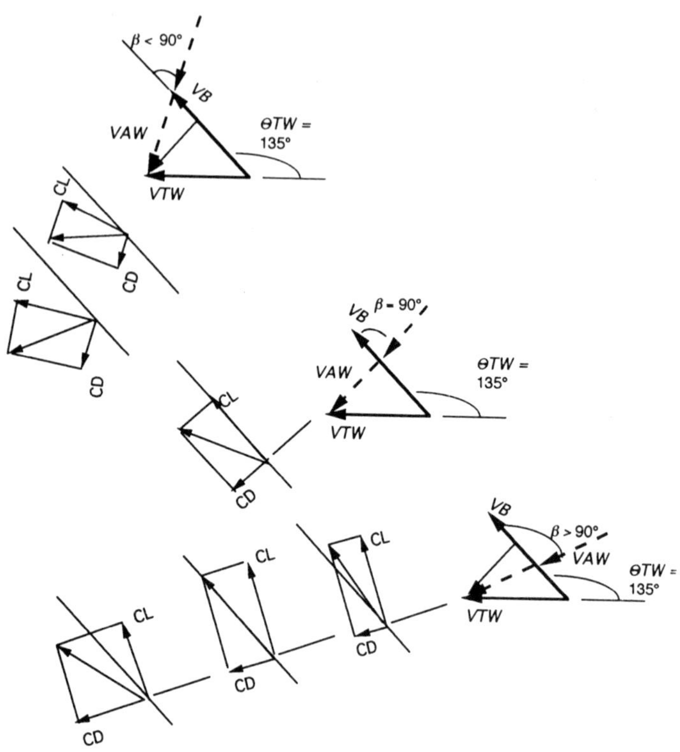


Figure 3-11
Some Possible $(C_D/C_L)$ Ratios for Boat Speeds Corresponding to ß>90°, ß=90° and ß<90°. θTW = 135°.

It is clear that at $ß = 90°$, the drag coefficient is the only component of driving force causing righting moment required (for rotation about the *VB* axis) so that minimizing $(C_D/C_L)$ while maximizing $C_L$ maximizes the driving force per pound displacement. If $C_D$ and $C_L$ are increased together while maintaining $C_D/C_L$, B/H will increase and so will the driving force per pound displacement. Such considerations are what the hypothetical ancient and modern sailmakers in Chapter 12 ponder.

Figure 3-12 displays similar $C_D/C_L$, $ß$, and *VB* combinations as for Figure 3-11, but for a deeper sailing true wind course angle of 165°. The same comments regarding when to use Equation (1A) or Equation (6) for $\ominus TW = 135°$ apply to Figure 3-12 and $\ominus TW = 165°$. For direct downwind ($\ominus TW = 180°$), it is better to use Equation (1A) for driving forces since $|C_H|$ is often 0 and $C_F -> C_D$. For most courses and boat speeds, where $ß$ is equal to or less than 90°, it is much preferred to use the raw wind forces as generated by equation (6), or its equivalent, equation (5), to represent the driving forces of the wind.

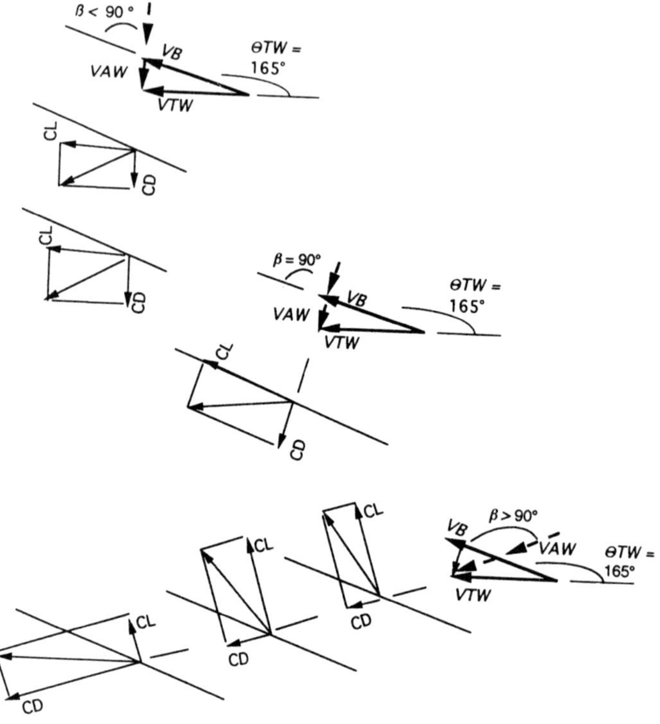


Figure 3-12
Some Possible $(C_D/C_L)$ Ratios for Boat Speeds Corresponding to
ß > 90°, ß = 90° and ß < 90°. $\Theta TW$ = 165°.

Since the speeds attainable for many sailboats on most courses result in an apparent wind angle, ß, that is equal to or less than 90°, the remainder of the treatise emphasizes the primitive result of Equation (6) with the further development of the LH side of Equation (4) and with example applications of the general theory to modern sailboats, boats of antiquity and non-flapping stoneflies of nature. The application to boats of antiquity in Chapter 12 concludes with a page from the hypothetical ancient sailmakers notebook. The next chapter presents an overview of the RH sides of the equations of motion.

# Chapter 4 - Right Hand Sides
## of the Equations of Motion

This chapter presents an overview of the Right Hand (RH) sides of Equations 4, 2, and 3 that define sailboat motions for smooth waters. The RH sides, two translational and one rotational, are the response sides to the LH sides of the Equations.

|  | Air | Water |  |
|---|---|---|---|
| Translation in direction of motion, $VB$ | $\eta\, F_{adf}$ = | $F_{wrf}$ | (4) |
| Translation perpendicular to direction of motion |  | $F_{ahf}$ = $F_{whf}$ | (2) |
| Rotation about axis in direction of motion | $M_{ahm}$ = | $M_{wrm}$ | (3) |

There is nothing new in the chapter and those familiar with total resistance and its components for a sailboat, leeway resistance, and all the forms possible for righting moment can skip this chapter. However, some things are different and are important in understanding the sailboat later on.

One difference is that upright hull resistance, $R_{up}$, is not partitioned into wave and skin friction components. Rather, it is simply, $R_{up}$. For many investigators, resistance is partitioned into parts associated with the posture a sailboat may take as it traverses a course on smooth waters. There is a separate component for angle of heel for example. That type of decomposition of total resistance is not new. Many theorists (for instance, Bradfield, 1980) make this type of component decomposition. The RH sides are addressed here in reverse order, beginning with the roll equation.

The Roll Equation

Equation (3) is the roll equation; that is, rotation about the axis of direction of motion ($VB$).

$$M_{ahf} = M_{wrm} \tag{3}$$

The RH side responds to overturning moments from aerodynamic force sources of the LH side. The righting moment available develops when the following situations occur: 1) when the center of gravity of the sailboat and the center of buoyancy separate on heeling (see Figure 4-1a and Figure 4-1b), 2) when static and dynamic flows of water produce pressure differentials on the hull and hulls at rest or in motion, or 3) when pressure differentials are produced by different lifts on supporting hydrofoils of hydrofoil craft (see Figure 4-1c), 4) when moveable ballast is moved side to side as in sandbagging or when crew weight is distributed from side to side in the sailboat underway (see Figure 4-1d), or when any combination of these occur as in Figure 4-1e. From whatever the righting moment comes, it can be used in the theory.

The total righting moment from all sources can be represented by the vessel displacement weight times a single equivalent righting arm for each speed attained by the vessel. The RH side of Equation (3) is a direct part of the definition of the modulating function for vessels in general and for vessels specifically when it represents the righting moment available. It is always turned into the form of $\Delta \times arm$, for the righting moment available in the modulating function of the theory.

The Side Force Equation

Equation (2) represents the force balance for the translational motion perpendicular to forward motions, $VB$.

$$F_{ahf} = F_{whf} \tag{2}$$

This balance of forces is for sideways motion, sometimes called sideslip or leeway, as opposed to headway motion. In almost every sailing direction, the aerodynamic driving forces on the sails are accompanied by sideways forces that pull the craft sideways to the direction the boat is headed. These sideways forces also heel the boat. In steady motion, the sideways flow of water, or the developed cross-flow, produces lift forces on the hull and keel appendages. These forces balance the sideways pull of the aerodynamic forces on the sail-rig (see Figure 4-2).

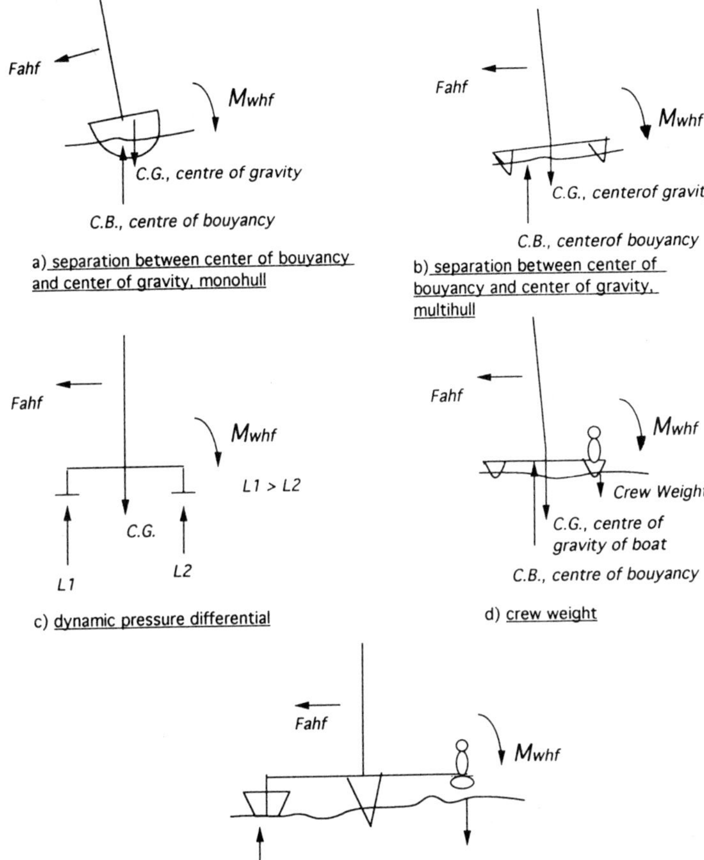


Figure 4-1
Possible Sources of Righting Moment

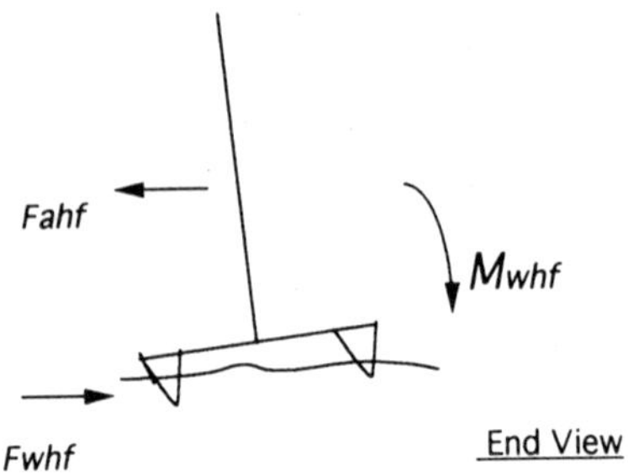
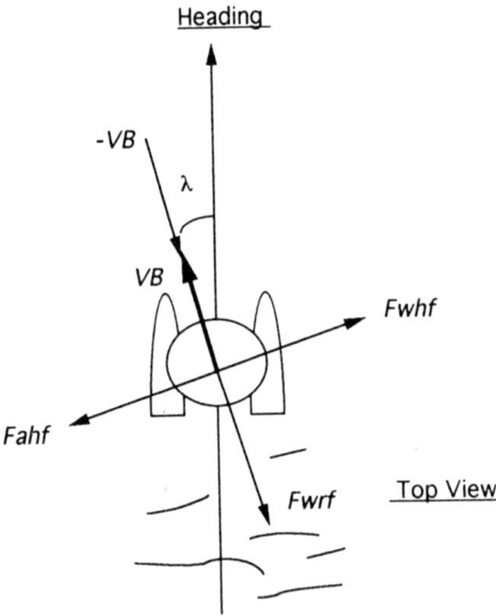


Figure 4-2
Leeway Angle for Developing a Balancing Side Force, $F_{whf}$

54

The leeway angle occurs for a fixed symmetrical lifting surface keel in order to generate the necessary balancing lift forces for steady forward motion. When the leeway angle is combined with lift and drag angles for the sail and hull, the combination is often the basis for other current and past theories (see discussion in Chapter 9). In the theory described here, the leeway angle is recognized through induced drag from necessary lift on the keel before the equilibrium speed of Equation (4) is found. It is used in estimated form for initial estimates of attached and separated flow drag from the appendages in the total resistance of Equation (4) when applied to specific boats. A steady leeway angle, $\lambda$, is what results in a balance to Equation (2) at steady course, $\theta TW$, and steady boat speed $VB$.

Total Resistance

The RH side of Equation (4) is the total resistance, $R_T$, in the direction of motion $VB$.

$$\eta\, F_{adf} = R_T \tag{4}$$

When using the raw wind charts from the theory, total resistance includes the resistance of the upright hull, $R_{up}$, plus appendage drag with attached flow, $R_{appatt}$, and appendage drag with separated flow, $R_{appsep}$, and hull heeled resistance increment, $R_h$, plus induced drag from the appendages (keel and rudder), $R_{indkeel}$, plus windage drag on the hull topsides (hull sides above water) and deck and deckhouse, $R_{windage}$. In symbol form, $R_T$ is written as

$$R_T = R_{up} + R_{appatt} + R_{appsep} + R_h + R_{indkeel} + R_{windage} \tag{9}$$

In the theory solution of Equation (4), all resistances are written as resistance per pound displacement weight (see Figure 4-3).

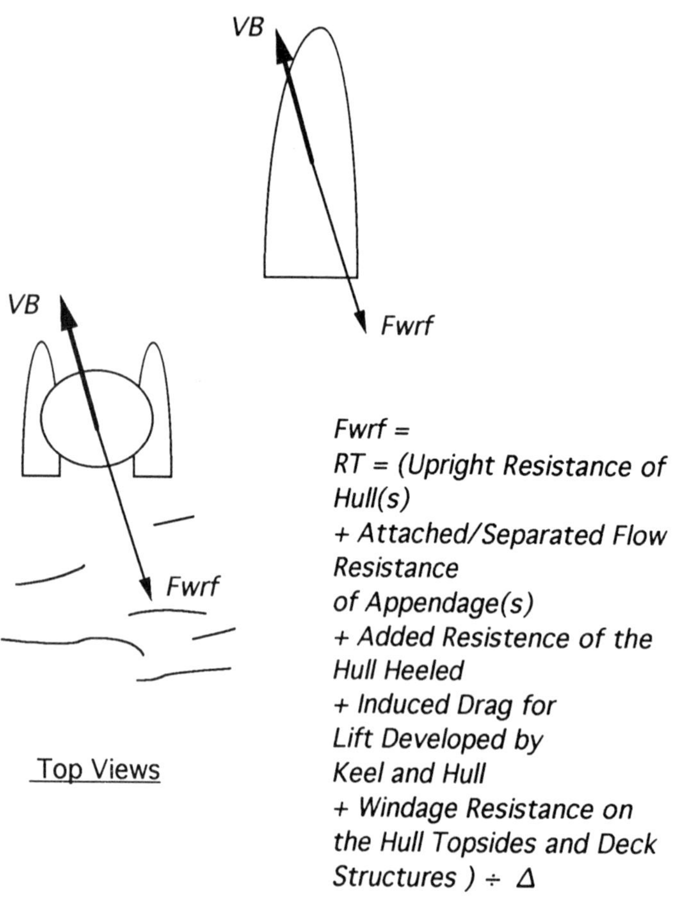


Figure 4-3
Total Resistance for Raw Wind Force Charts

56

Upright Hull Resistance

Upright resistance for specific hulls can be represented by a frictional component and a wave component, plus a component to represent separated flow on the hull. The components then add up to the total upright resistance. This is often the current practice. The wave resistance is related to a length Froude number, and the frictional resistance is related to a Reynolds number. The literature is full of frictional coefficient and wave coefficient estimates for specific hulls. There is less published information that estimates, or which is used to estimate, the appropriate hull resistance coefficient for separated flow, even with high-power computer based, fluid-flow-coded model results, and even though the problem dates back to 1914 with Prandtl (Schlichting, 1968, p. 3). Upright resistance is discussed in Chapter 7 and is presented in a convenient form, backed by theory and experiment, that contains wave and frictional resistance implicitly and represents explicitly total resistance bounds for many upright hull forms.

Appendage Resistance, Separated and Attached Flows

Part of Appendage Resistance, $R_{app}$, is independent of lift. The part of $R_{app}$ that is independent from lift exists even when lift is zero. There are two ways of representing this resistance. One uses wetted surface area as a reference area and is more complex than the way of representation used here. Here $R_{app}$ is taken in a form that uses the frontal area as the reference area. Frontal area is defined as frontal area per pound displacement weight in order to preserve resistance per pound displacement when related to water flow kinetic energy densities like $q_w$ in Equation (10) below. Two types of flow, attached and separated, can occur over the appendage surfaces (see Figure 4-4).

The significant difference in drag from attached flow and separated flow on sailboat appendages has been recognized at least since 1961 in the world of sailboats. George B. Moffat, Jr. (Moffat, Robinson, Moffat, 1961) says, "Centerboards and rudders tend to stall easily whenever the angle of attack—that is, angle at which the surface meets the water—gets over eight degrees.

At the stalling point the drag increases enormously since the surface becomes very inefficient." (Full stall flow is the same as fully separated flow.)

The leeway angle, $\lambda$, indicates the degree of separated flow over appendages for example applications of the theory. At $\lambda < 5°$, flow is considered fully attached, and at $\lambda > 25°$, flow is considered fully separated with the corresponding coefficients shown below as 0.1 and 1.0. This part of total resistance is shown in symbol form in Equation (10):

$$R_{app}/\Delta = C_d\, q_w\, (A_{ref}/\Delta) \tag{10}$$

where

$R_{app}$ = appendage resistance independent of induce drag
      resistance
$C_d$ attached = 0.1
$C_d$ fully separated = 1.0
$q_w$ = 1/2 $\rho_w$ $VB^2$
$A_{ref}$ = frontal area of the appendage
$\rho_w$ = density of water
$\Delta$ = displacement weight of vessel

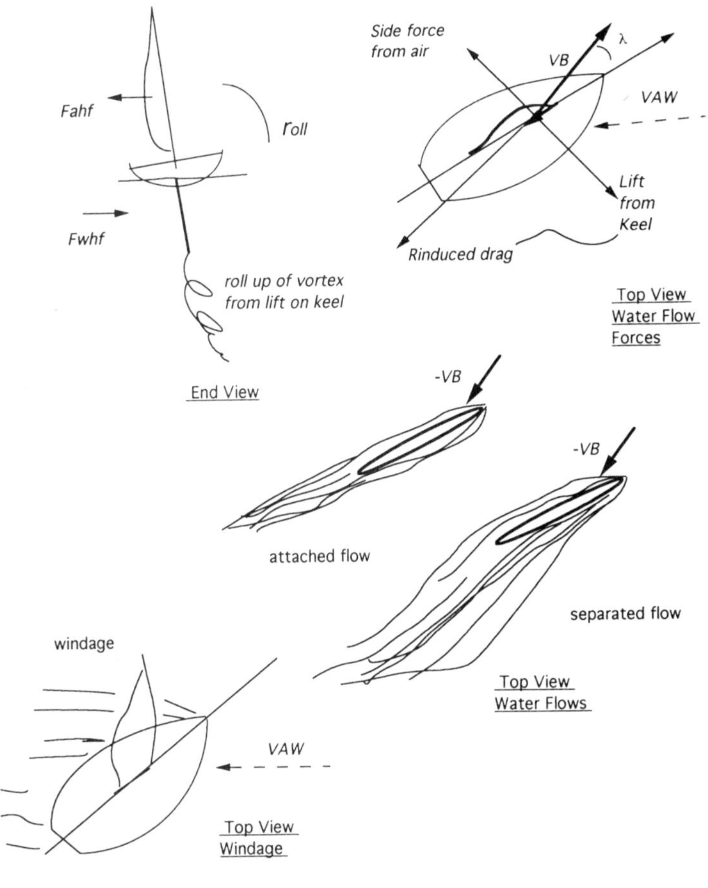



Figure 4-4
Attached and Separated Flows on Appendages
with Top View of Windage on the Topsides of the Hull

59

For specific vessel applications, $\lambda$ may be less than 5° or greater than 25° or between 5° and 25°.

Induced Drag Resistance from the Appendages

Induced drag resistance from the appendages is drag related to the lift produced by the appendages. It is taken in its first form below as used by Hoerner (1965), while Kerwin (1978) replaces the factor 1/2 with 1/1.72, and Marchaj (1964) replaces 1/2 with 1/1.7.

$$R_{ind} = (1/\pi)\ (1/q_w)\ (1/2)\ (lift^2/T^2) \times (1/\Delta) \qquad (11)$$

where

$$q_w = 1/2\ \rho_w\ VB^2$$
$$T = \text{the span of the keel}$$
$$\rho_w = \text{density of water}$$

Most investigators use this form of Equation (11) as the starting point for representations of the induced drag for the sailboat underway (see Figure 4-4). In the next chapter, where the defining of Available Wind Force (AWF) occurs, induced drag is converted to a form compatible with $B/H$ and Raw Wind Force.

Windage Drag

Drag from aerodynamic flows on topsides parts (parts above the water line from side to side) of the hull not directly associated with the production of the driving forces is called windage drag. It can be represented as the sum of drags from individual topsides and deck components with bluff body and frictional drag theories and data for specific boats from models; see, for example, Hoerner (1965). Individual components may include the deck house, winches, tracks, dorades, etc. When such drag is used in the theory, it is always represented as per pound displacement drag for specific vessels and for vessels in general. A special form for windage is derived and used in the theory. It is shown in the next chapter.

Thus total resistance for raw wind charts of the general theory includes drag or resistance from all sources. The leeway angle is an important part of the RH side of the sideways motion equation. Righting moment for the roll equation of motion is from all sources.

In the next chapter, raw wind forces of the LH side are modified by wind-related parts of total resistance of the Right Hand side in the further development of the theory for understanding the sailboat.

# Chapter 5 - Available Wind Forces

Available Wind Forces

The definition of available wind force (AWF) in this chapter recognizes that some revised scientific mathematical accounting procedures can help in the understanding of the sailboat in the context of the theory. The revised accounting procedures may explode some myths, especially those of some RH side, response traditionalists who embrace the idea that sailboat speed is limited by hull speed alone (the sharp upturn of a resistance curve with speed), and further hold tightly to the idea that all that is necessary to go faster is a little more hull speed, or a little more wind, or more sail! There are advances in the understanding of the sailboat in this chapter. Resistance parts of the RH side of Equation (4) that are attributable to the wind are transferred to the LH side of (4). The result is that, for sailboats under control, there is slightly less force than the raw wind forces of Chapter 3 to drive vessels and their crew to yet faster speeds.

The LH side of Equation (1) was modified in Chapter 3 with a free modulating function to produce Equation (4). The raw wind forces of Equation (8) are the LH side of (4).

$$\text{Air} \quad \text{Water}$$

Translation in the direction
of motion, $VB$
$$\eta\, F_{adf} = F_{wrf} \qquad (4)$$

$$\eta\, F_{adf} = (B/H)\ (C_F/C_H)\ (1/2\mu) =$$

$$(B/H)\ \frac{[\sin(\beta) - (C_D/C_L)\cos(\beta)]}{[\cos(\beta) + (C_D/C_L)\sin(\beta)]}\ (1/2\mu) \qquad (8)\ ****$$

The LH side of Equation (1) is to be further modified here. Raw wind forces per pound displacement from (8) for the sailboat underway are modified by windage and induced drag resistance by a transfer of these direct-wind-related drag resistances. Windage drag and induced keel drag are transferred from the RH side of Equation (4) to the LH side. This results in a definition of Available Wind Force that is slightly less than raw wind forces for most true wind courses and speeds.

Available Wind Force is defined as Raw Wind Force of Equation (8) minus windage, $F_{windage}$, and minus induced drag from lift on the keel, $F_{indkeel}$. It is shown in Equation (12):

$$\text{Available Wind Force} = \text{Raw Wind Force} - F_{windage} - F_{indkeel} \qquad (12)$$

where all forces are per pound displacement.

It should be noted that the induced drag from aerodynamic lift on the sails is included in the drag part of the drag to lift ratio that is defined for the sail-rig combination that produces the driving forces in Equation (8). The induced drag resistance in Equation (12) is different. It is from the lift on the keel in the water in response to the sideways forces of the sails in the air above the water.

The new set of equations to be solved in an equilibrium of boat speed for smooth water conditions for any sailboat are now,

Translation in direction
of motion, VB
$$\eta\, F_{adf} - F_{windage} - F_{indkeel} = \underline{F}_{wrf} \qquad (13)$$

Translation perpendicular to direction
of motion, VB
$$F_{ahf} = F_{whf} \qquad (2)$$

Rotation about axis in direction
of motion, VB
$$M_{ahf} = M_{wrm} \qquad (3)$$

The underline in $\underline{F}_{wrf}$ indicates that $\underline{F}_{wrf}$ is the total resistance associated with Available Wind Force. Forms for representation of windage and induced drags compatible with the theory are presented next.

Windage

A frontal area model is used to estimate windage drag with a separated drag coefficient of 1 assumed. Recent work (see Blount and Bartee, 1997, p. 280) indicates this coefficient may be as low as 0.5 for sleek craft topsides. The windage force is opposite to the direction of motion $VB$. So windage is the cosine of the apparent wind angle $ß$ times the windage drag force in the direction of the apparent wind, $VAW$.

$$windage/\Delta = C_{dfrontal}\ A_{frontal}\ (1/\Delta)\ \cos ß\ q_a \qquad (14)$$

The frontal area of the topsides is approximated for small $\lambda(\lambda < 2°)$ as $A_{lateral} \times \sin ß$ (see Figure 5-1).

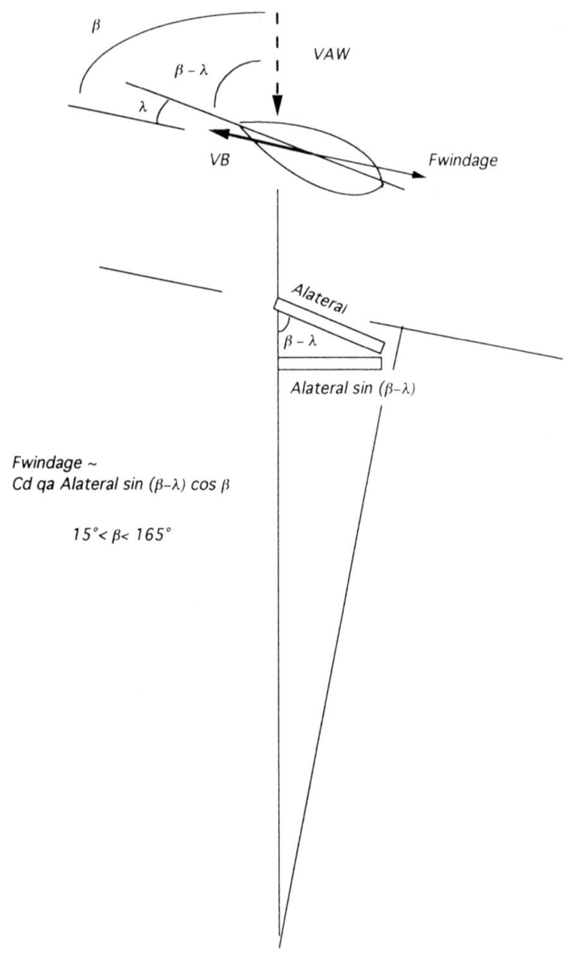


Figure 5-1
Windage Force, Representation

When the frontal area is approximated in this form the boat parameter is projected topsides-lateral area (ft^2) per pound displacement and it is multiplied by cos ß, sin ß and $q_a$, the kinetic energy density of the air to produce windage in a form compatible with the theory, as follows:

$$\text{windage}/\Delta = (A_{lateral}/\Delta) \sin (ß - \lambda) \, q_a \, \cos ß \quad (ß - \lambda > 15°) \quad (15)$$

$$\sim (A_{lateral}/\Delta) \sin (ß) \, q_a \, \cos ß \quad (ß > 15°, \lambda = 0)$$

where
$$q_a = 1/2 \, \rho_a \, VAW^2, \text{ and}$$
$$\rho_a = \text{density of air}$$

One remarkable attribute when it is taken in this form is that sin ß cos ß reflects accurately the change in sign from negative to positive for the effect of windage on the driving force that occurs when windage goes from aft the beam (ß > 90°) as speed picks up to forward of the beam (ß < 90°). When it is aft the beam, it is an addition to the driving force. ($A_{lateral}/\Delta$ is different for each boat but is taken as 0.015 ft²/lb for estimating windage for the limit boat speeds of Chapter 9.) The effect of windage on *AWF* for *ƟTW* > 90° is seen in Figures 5-4 and 5-5.

Induced Drag Resistance

Induced drag resistance is developed from the lift on the keel in response to the heeling forces on the rig (see Figure 5-2).

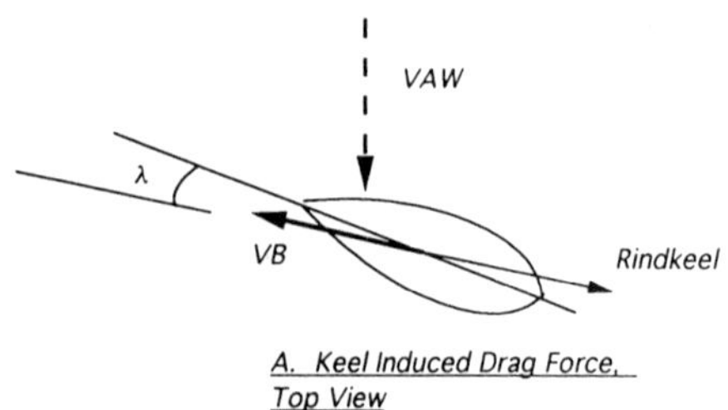


A. Keel Induced Drag Force,
Top View

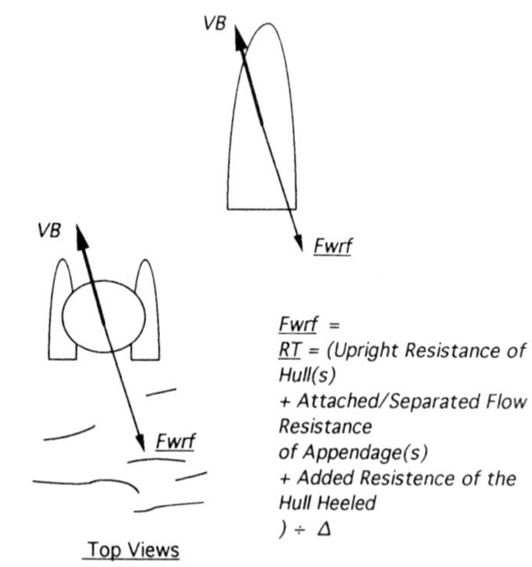


B. Total Resistance for Available Wind Force

Figure 5-2
A. Induced Drag Force
B. Total Resistance for Available Wind Force

Induced drag resistance on the keel is taken from Hoerner (1965, p. 7-2) as

$$R_{indkeel} = (1/\pi)\,(1/q_w)\,(1/2T)\hat{\,}2 \times (lift\hat{\,}2)\,(1/\Delta) \qquad (16)$$

where

$$q_w = 1/2 \times \rho_w \times VB\hat{\,}2$$
$$T = \text{the span of the keel}$$
$$\rho_w = \text{density of water}$$

This form is used by most investigators. The factor 1/2 is some-times taken as 1/1.72 by Kerwin (1978) or 1/1.7 by Marchaj (1964) to represent the starting point for representations of the induced drag resistance for the sailboat under way.

When the lift on the keel is set equal to the heel force on the sails and the geometric aspect ratio (ARGK) of the keel is used and 1/2 B as the maximum heeling arm is used, it is found by using Equation (3) that

$$R_{indkeel} = (1/\pi)\,(1/q_w)\,(1/2)\,(1/2\mu)\hat{\,}2\,(B/H)\hat{\,}2$$

$$(S.A./A_{keel})\,(1/S.A./\Delta)(1/ARGK) \qquad (17)$$

where

$$ARGK = T\hat{\,}2/A_{keel}$$
$$T = \text{span of the keel}$$
$$A_{keel} = \text{area of the keel (lateral area of one side)}$$
$$S.A. = \text{planform sail area}$$
$$\Delta = \text{displacement weight of vessel}$$
$$B/H = \text{theory parameter}$$

When $ARGK$ is set equal to 3.5, $\mu = 0.4$, and $(S.A./A_{keel})$ is set equal to 100 (Norwood, 1979 p.51, uses 67 for fast sailboats), then $R_{indkeel}$ becomes

$$7.1 \times (1/q_w) \times (B/H)\hat{\,}2 \times (1/(S.A./\Delta)) \qquad (18)$$

Thus an approximation for Available Wind Forces (AWF) for an efficient high-speed sailboat

($\lambda \sim 0°$) is

$$(B/H) (C_F/C_H) (1/.8) - (Alateral/\Delta) \sin ß \quad q_a \cos ß$$

$$-7.1 (1/q_w) (B/H)\char94 2 (1/(S.A./\Delta)) \qquad (19)$$

Examples of charts for Available Wind Force for a high-speed vessel capable of sailing at a $B/H$ of 0.8, with a slick rig-sail combination that achieves a lift to drag ratio of 0.15 and $S.A./\Delta$ ratio of 0.4 ft^2/lb and has an $A_{lateral}/\Delta$ ratio of 0.015 ft^2/lb in 30 knots of true wind are shown. For a course of $\ominus TW$ = 45° see Figure 5-3. For a course of $\ominus TW$ = 110°, a high-speed heading, see Figure 5-4. For a course of $\ominus TW$ = 135°, another high-speed heading, see Figure 5-5. In these charts leeway angle $\lambda$ is defined as zero, $\lambda$ = 0, and sailtrim angle $\delta$ is zero, $\delta$ = 0, or is such that $C_D/C_L$ for the sails set applies.

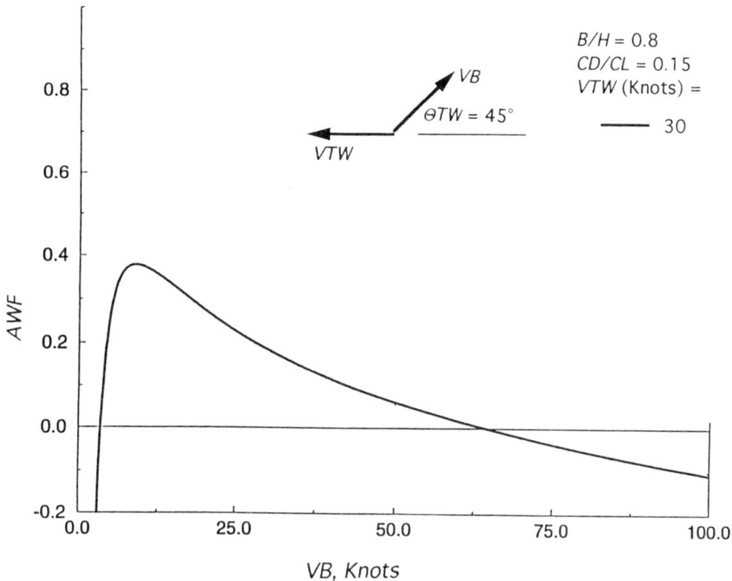


Figure 5-3
$\Theta TW = 45°$ Available Wind Force, $S.A./A_{keel} = 100$,
$S.A./\Delta = 0.4$ ft^2/lb, $A_{lateral}/\Delta = 0.015$ ft^2/lb, $\lambda = 0°$

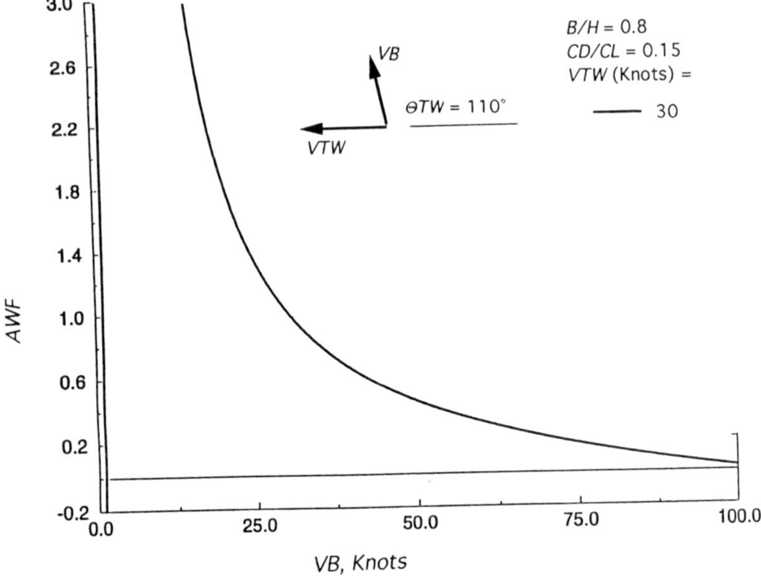



Figure 5-4

$\theta TW = 110°$ Available Wind Force, $S.A./A_{keel} = 100$, $S.A./\Delta = 0.4$ ft^2/lb, $A_{lateral}/\Delta = 0.015$ ft^2/lb, $\lambda = 0°$

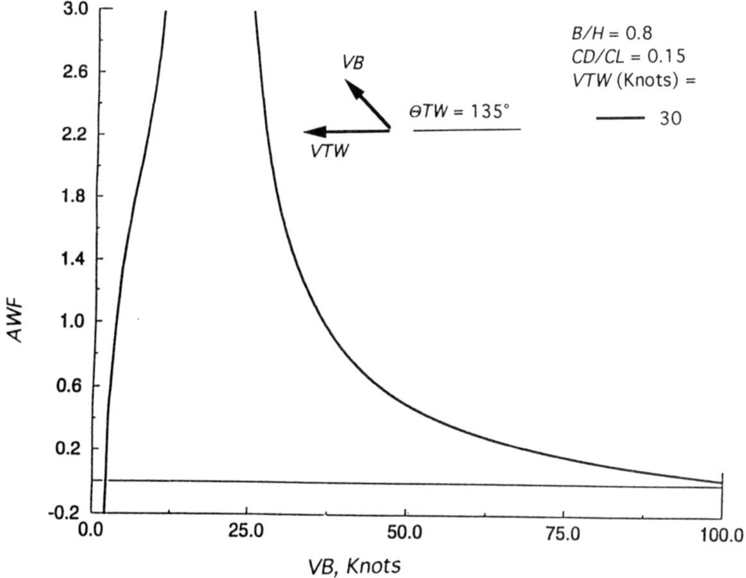


Figure 5-5
$\theta TW = 135°$ Available Wind Force, $S.A./A_{keel} = 100$,
$S.A./\Delta = 0.4$ ft^2/lb, $A_{lateral}/\Delta = 0.015$ ft^2/lb, $\lambda = 0°$

The negative value of available driving force at near zero speed is due to the high induced drag resistance at near zero speed. In fact, the boat is normally operated at a smaller $B/H$ in this region with proportionally less driving force but picking up $B/H$ and driving forces as it goes to increased speeds. What Figure 5-3 for $\Theta TW = 45°$ does show is part of the reason why it is very difficult to start a sailboat off from rest at $\Theta TW = 45°$ even if the sails are trimmed. Such an exercise produces a lot of sideways movement from high induced drag resistance, not to mention slowness from separated flow drag also. It is much better to sail a boat cross wind at approximately $\Theta TW = 110°$, pick up speed, then come up to weather course of $\Theta TW = 45°$. Such a technique is what most sailors (yachtsmen and yachtswomen and sailboarders) use most of the time for getting underway.

Chapter 8 on specific sailboat applications gives examples for permitting $B/H$ and $C_D/C_L$ ratios to be a function of boat speed and $\beta$, the apparent wind angle. Then AWF starts at $VAW = VTW$ with zero boat speed and increases smoothly and continuously before decreasing to its limit point at high boat speed. The highest boat speed potential of zero resistance is not realized because the resistance forces in the RH side of Equation (13) are generally greater than zero and rise with speed to intercept Available Wind Force in a real-time equilibrium boat speed, $VB_{equilibrium}$.

It is worthwhile noting again that the Available Wind Charts shown here represent driving forces for a sailboat already sailing at the $B/H$ ratio of the chart for each speed. At low speed, $1/q_w$ is very large, hence the large negative value for the charted expression that includes low speed induced drag resistance at high $B/H$ or $B/H > 0.0$.

The spikes in Figure 5-4 for $\Theta TW = 110°$ and in Figure 5-5 for $\Theta TW = 135°$ occur because as the boat moves along the $VB$ line, increasing in speed towards its eventual equilibrium speed, the apparent wind angle transitions from abaft beam amidship where $\beta$ is greater than $90°$ to forward beamamidship where $VAW$ strikes the sails at a $\beta$ less than $90°$. The transition from $\beta > 90°$ to $\beta < 90°$ is near the boat speed where the spike occurs for true wind courses greater than 90° and less than 165° (*near ß = 90°, ($C_F$ /$C_H$) -> 1 ÷ ($C_D$ /$C_L$)).* The boat sailing in these charts is for $C_D$ /$C_L$ = 0.15. Such a boat has a full-swivel sail such as is used on a sailboard! It is for a boat where the sail trim angle, $\delta$, is continually adjusted to make high speed $C_D$ /$C_L$ ratios true. At the higher speeds, $\delta$ is zero.

It is clear from these figures that the actual force available to drive a sailboat to its eventual speed is less than the Raw Wind Forces of the fundamental result of the general theory. Available Wind Force is the "realistic" wind force available to drive the sailboat that arises at equilibrium speed, *VB*, of point $P_i$. When $P_i$ is expanded to a sailboat in three geometric dimensions, 3-D, then is produced another sailboat concept for launching on the waters of the earth. (Such is what is meant by the title of the unpublished manuscript (1989) which first described the core of the discovery herein, "Out of the Fifth Dimension, Into the Third and Onto the Fourth.")

The new understandings in this chapter are that the character of the wind's forces for a sailboat in control is very important in determining its speed on smooth waters, and that there is slightly less force than the Raw Wind Forces of Chapter 3 to drive the sailboat (both sailboats of antiquity and sailboats of today) to faster speeds yet! This chapter thus advances the understanding of the theory and the sailboat. Available Wind Force narrows further one side of the boundaries that define the envelope boundaries for sailboat speed.

The next chapter presents some theorems and proofs based on the theory for the sailboat. Then Chapter 7 links upright resistance to hull form and places a lower bound on total resistance for use with available wind charts. That lower bound is used in Chapter 9 to find the limits to upright sailboat speed on smooth waters.

# Chapter 6 - Three Theorems, a Lemma and Proofs

This chapter presents theorems and proofs related to the results of the general theory. Most readers can skip this chapter. However, it does emphasize that equilibrium boat speed in the general theory is the intersection of a LH side-driving force curve and a RH side resistance force curve.

Equations (6) for Raw Wind Forces ($RAWF$) and (12) for Available Wind Forces ($AWF$) are regarded as generating functions. What this means is that when given the variables $B/H$, $VTW$, $\ominus TW$, $\mu$, and form for $C_F$ and $C_H$, then the expressions generate a driving force per pound displacement for the sailboat at each $VB$.

$$RAWF = (B/H) \, (C_F/C_H) \, (1/2\mu) \qquad\qquad (6)$$

$$AWF = RAWF - Windage/\Delta -$$
$$induced \; drag \; resistance \; of \; keel/\Delta \qquad\qquad (12)$$

These expressions apply to $\ominus TW$ when it is less than about 170°. (For direct downwind, $\ominus TW = 180°$, and the generating function for $RAWF$ is, $RAWF = C_F \, q_a \, (S.A./\Delta)$ with $VAW = (VTW - VB)$, and $C_F$ is nearly equal to 1, where $q_a = 1/2 \, \rho a VAW^2$, $\rho a$ = density of air).

For a set of variables related to a class of sailboats or to a specific sailboat, Equations *(6) and (12) generate curves of driving forces* for the vessels. When these are coupled with resistance curves corresponding to the class of sailboats or specific sailboats, the resistance curves produce predicted boat speeds for the vessels. The predicted speeds are at the resistance curve's intersection with the driving force curves.

The following theorems and lemma state this in a formal way. Theorem 1 represents the convergence of boat speed, $VB$, to $VB_{equilibrium}$ with $RAWF$. Lemma 1 represents the convergence to boat speed with $AWF$. Theorem 2 relates to maximum driving forces for a vessel with $RAWF$. Theorem 3 relates to maximum driving forces with $AWF$. An important assumption in all these theorems is that acceleration of the point that represents the sailboat is in the same line as *VB* and when the acceleration force balance reverses itself with its sign, then *VB* expands or contracts accordingly along the same line. Another assumption in these proofs is that an intersection exists and at an intersection of resistance and driving force curves the driving force curve is a decreasing function of *VB* and resistance is an increasing function of *VB* or resistance is increasing faster than the driving force.

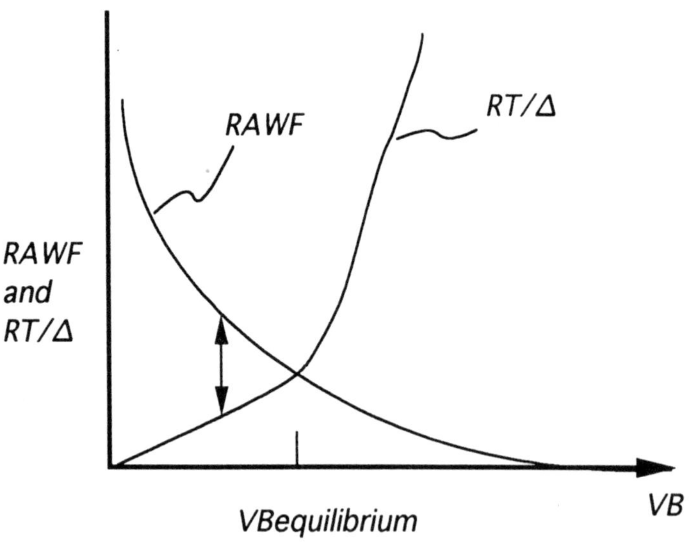



Figure 6-1
*VB* Increases Until I -> 0

Theorem 1. When underway, a boat, capable of sailing at a $B/H$ > 0 for a Raw Wind Course $\theta TW$, will converge to a boat speed, $VB_{equilibrium}$ corresponding to the intersection of the vessel's resistance curve with the Raw Wind Force curve (see Figure 6-1). That is, $VB$ increases until
$\delta (F/\Delta) = (F_{raw/\Delta} - R_T/\Delta) \to 0$. Given: $B/H$ > 0 for $t$ > 0, $VB_j = VB_i + \delta VB_i$, $j = i + 1$, $i = $ instant $t_i$.


a.  Acceleration, $a_i = \delta(F/\Delta) \times g$, $\delta VB_i = a_i \times \delta t_i$
b.  $\delta (F/\Delta)$ > 0 => $a_i$ > 0 => $\delta VB_i$ > 0 and $VB_j > VB_i$
c.  $VB_j$ continues to increase until at $VB_{equilibrium}$ $F_{raw}/\Delta = R_T/\Delta$,
    $(F_{raw}/\Delta - R_T/\Delta) = 0$, $a_i = 0$,
    $\delta VB_i = 0$ and $VB_j = VB_i$  Q.E.D.


Lemma 1. When Available Wind Force of Equation (12) rather than Raw Wind Force is taken as the driving force for the vessel, then a Total Resistance Curve that does not include induced drag resistance or windage is applied to the charted curve (see Figure 6-2). If the vessel is capable of sailing at the $B/H$ of the chart curve and the windage and induced drag resistance reflect the actual vessel or class of vessel, then from rest, the vessel will increase speed to converge to an equilibrium boat speed where $(F_{awf}/\Delta - R_T/\Delta) = 0$.

The proof is similar to that for Theorem 1.

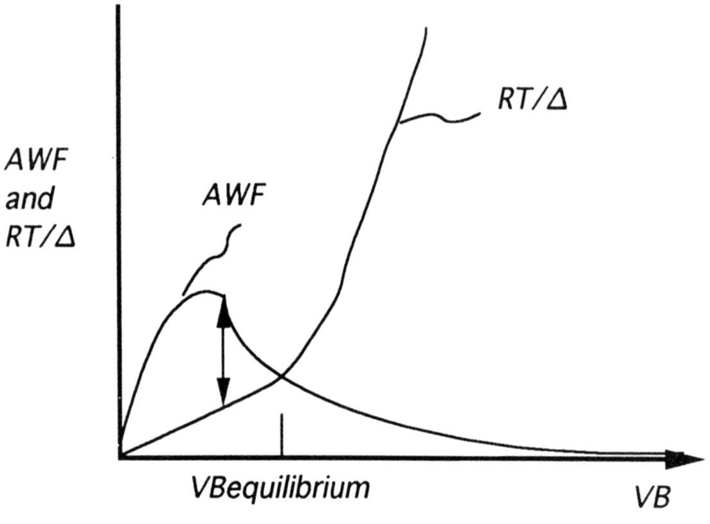



Figure 6-2
*AWF, VB* Increases Until $\updownarrow$ -> 0

Theorem 2.  Assuming $C_F/C_H$ is the same at each *VB*, then Equation (6) for Raw Wind Force represents maximum driving forces for a vessel sailing at a specified *B/H* with windage near zero and induced drag resistance near zero (see Figure 6-3). This is an unlikely situation for individual sailboats for the range of *VB* from 0 to 100 knots.

    a. $(B/H)(C_F/C_H)(1/2\mu)$ is the driving force per pound displacement.
    b. The vessel sails at maximum $B/H = (B/H)_1$
       or $(B/H)_2 < (B/H)_1$
    c. $\mu$ is a function of angle of heel, $C_D/C_L$ is a function of ß
    d. $C_F/C_H \equiv (sinß - C_D/C_L\ cosß) \div (cosß + C_D/C_L\ sinß)$
    e. At each *VB* of *RAWF*, ß, and $C_F/C_H$, and $(1/2\mu)$ are the same for a given vessel.
    f. *RAWF1* > *RAWF2*  Q.E.D.

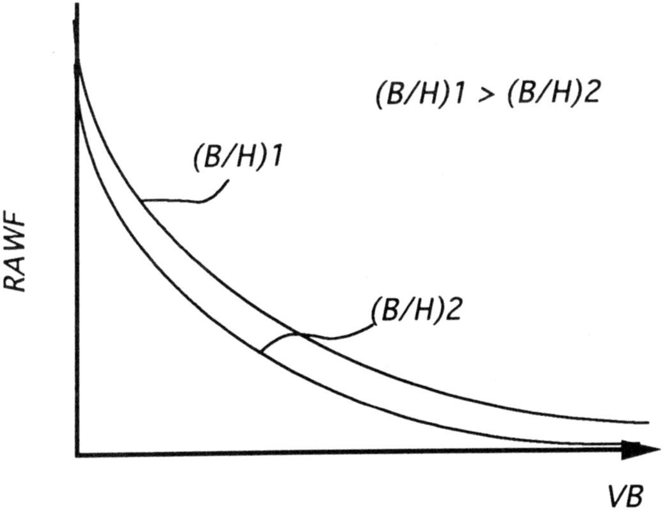


Figure 6-3
Maximum Driving Force for a Given ⊝TW

No theorem is written for maximum available wind force since windage and induced drag resistance are vessel specific and may cause maximum *AWF* to fluctuate between two *B/H* for a range of *VB*, for an non-upright boat. Windage can be estimated with angle of heel, but induced drag resistance is difficult to define for the heeled boat.  See Figure 6-4.

The next theorem proves the equivalence of Raw Wind Force for catamarans and monohulls, even those not at hull-afly angles of righting moment arm.

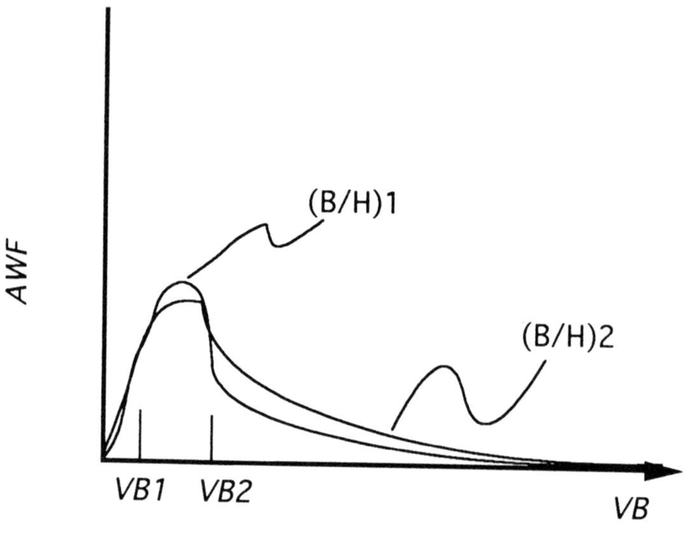


Figure 6-4
Maximum *AWF* May Fluctuate with *B/H* and the Range of *VB* Sailed for Specific Vessels

Theorem 3.  While *B/H* is originally for a catamaran at hull-afly, the *RAWF* and *AWF* representations apply for any vessel for which an equivalent *B/H* can be defined.

    a.  2 *arm*$_i$/H (vessel specific) $= (B/H)_{equivalent}$
    b.  All else in the expression for Raw Wind Force is the same.

The examples in Chapters 8 and 10 for specific boats show how this is used.

This completes the general theory for smooth water. Charts of *RAWF* and *AWF* have been produced. They are firm strokes, noniterative curved slash marks on paper of an infinite string of possibilities as illustrated in Figure 6-5.

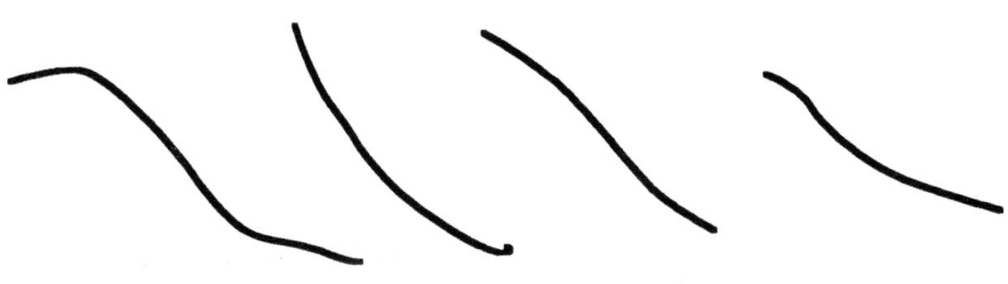

Figure 6-5
Noninterative Slash Marks Illustrate Driving Forces

Adding an ascending resistance curve slash mark to any of the descending driving force slash curves produces an equilibrium boat speed predictive of the class of sailboats or a sailboat in particular for a specified or expected leeway angle, sail trim angle, and ($C_D$ /$C_L$) ratios for a sail-rig representative of the sailboats.

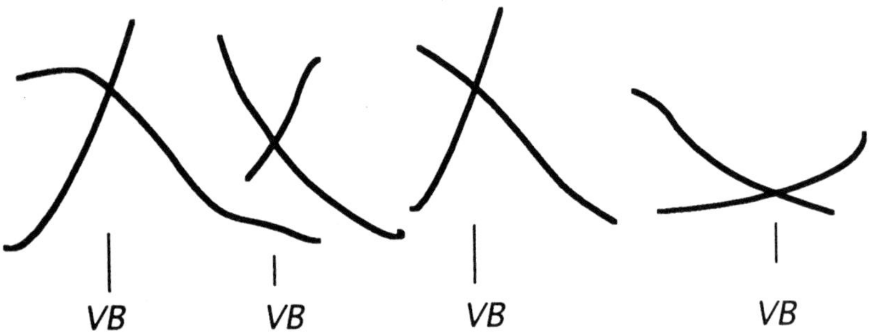



Figure 6-6
Two Slash Marks (One Driving Forces, One Resistance Forces)
Illustrate One Equilibrium Speed for Each Combination

Applications of the theory in Chapters 8-12 involve identifying the Available Wind Forces curves and appropriate resistance curves for smooth flat waters for the vessels in the applications. Chapter 7, next, presents accurate ways of linking hull form and posture to hull resistance for estimating total resistance for use with the general theory in the application examples.

# Chapter 7 - Total Resistance

In this chapter several ways are presented and reviewed to estimate hull and appendage resistance. The chapter emphasizes one special form of upright resistance representation for a range of hull forms and a range of speed possibilities from among the several resistance forms reviewed. The special form for hull resistance links general shape to resistance and speed. One of the "beauties" of the general theory presented here is that *RAWF* and *AWF* apply to however the resistance curve for a particular craft is estimated.

Identifying resistance to forward motion for sailboat hulls is the focus of many investigators in the past and present. Hulls have been and are powered by wooden paddle, by flaxen sail, by sail and long wooden oars, by oars and sail, by sail and expanding steam, by steam, by exploding diesel, and by hot nuclear power. How to specify the total resistance for a sailboat hull or any hull, however powered, is a subject that stems from antiquity. In antiquity resistance was most likely represented by "ancient seat of the pants" observations and judgments carried in the heads of early explorers, boat builders, designers, warriors, and empire builders. Full scale trial-and-error methods and rough judgments for assessing hull abilities continued up to the opening of the modern era of the scientific approach. The modern era brought William Froude's assumption of corresponding speeds for geosims of 1868 (PNA, 1988) and observations of wave resistance and frictional resistance for full-sized and model-sized hulls, followed by years with legions of tank test results from scientific experiments on series of hulls by David Taylor and K.S. Davidson and others during the early part of the 20th century. Still other contemporary naval architects/scientists continue to identify the "real-actual" resistance of hulls for sailboats, sailing yachts and sailing ship hulls with tank tested models.

By the time the early scientists began to look at hull resistance from more than a "seat of the pants" view, the age of sail had passed, having ended in about 1854 according to John Van Duyn Southworth in *The Age of Sails* (1968) with the advent of combined steam and sail power and then steam power replacing the sail power of the great ships of the line. Resistance identification for specific vessel's hull(s) is a subject of ongoing research today via towing tank models and hydrodynamic flow codes inserted into many variable computational models, where sometimes over 90 variables define the computational programs (Van Oossanen, 1993). The computational models are activated on super computers for hull form resistance corresponding to specific geometries. These computer programs can run for 24 hours and more before producing results that may or may not identify appropriate hull resistance. A good place for the reader to start in getting a feel for the history of total resistance and its forms of identification is with the references in the annotated bibliography (e.g., PNA, 1988, Marchaj, 1979, etc).

This chapter presents a reasonable basis for estimating the total resistance of most sharply pointed and smoothly shaped hulls with their appendages. It is based on knowing the length to volume to the one-third power ratio ($L/\forall^{1/3}$ ratio) for the hull(s) to start with. It uses the volume Froude number, $F\forall$, as the basic speed parameter for upright hull resistance. The volume Froude number is defined as the speed of the hull divided by the square root of the quantity formed by acceleration, $g$, times the cube root of the displacement volume, as shown in Equation (20).

$$F_\forall = VB \div (\sqrt{g \times \forall^{1/3}}) \tag{20}$$

where

$VB$ = speed of the hull
$g$ = acceleration of gravity
$\forall$ = Volume displacement corresponding to Archimedes'
      displacement

Since the Raw Wind Charts and Available Wind Charts are in pound force per pound of Archimedes' displacement weight, the resistance curves that are used in combination with the charts to predict resistance are necessarily in pound force per pound displacement weight. So resistance used with these charts, whatever its original units of measurement, is necessarily converted first to resistance (lbs) per vessel hull form displacement, $\Delta$, (lbs).

Total resistance, $\underline{R}_T$, is for use with Available Wind Force charts. It is,

$$\underline{R}_T = R_{up} + R_{appatt} + R_{appsep} + R_h \qquad (21)$$

where

$$\underline{R}_T = \underline{F}_{wrf}$$

Total resistance includes the resistance of the hull upright, $R_{up}$, plus appendage drag with attached flow, $R_{appatt}$, and appendage drag with separated flow, $R_{appsep}$, and hull heeled resistance increment, $R_h$. The heeled resistance is additional resistance for the hull when it leans a little as it traverses the smooth waters. These components that define total resistance are discussed one at a time.

Upright Resistance

It is common to view the upright resistance and heeled resistance to be produced by a wave-producing component, and a frictional (viscous) drag component, and a separated flow component:

$$R_{up} = R_{wave} + R_{friction} + R_{hullsep} \qquad (22)$$

or with the Froude assumption where residuary resistance is defined as wave-making resistance.

$$R_{up} = R_{residuary} + R_{friction} + R_{correction} \qquad (23)$$

where

$$R_{friction}/\Delta = C_{fric}(Rn) \times 0.5 \times F_v^2 \times (W.S. \div \forall^{2/3}) \qquad (24)$$

$C_{fric}\ (Rn)$ = Coefficient of friction as a function of Reynolds number

$Rn = VB \times L \div$ kinematic viscous coefficient for the fluid

*W.S.* = wetted surface

*L* = length; it may be waterline length or a % of waterline length

*Rn* approximately equals $4.59 \times F_v \times (L/\forall^{1/3}) \times \forall^{1/3} \times 10^5$ (25)

Sometimes for a class of hulls the $R_T/\Delta$ found is charted versus volume Froude number (*F∀*). Savitsky and Gore (1980) did this for a general class of semi-planning fast hulls according to different length to volume to the 1/3 power ratios $(L/\forall^{1/3})$, sometimes also called a fineness ratio. Their results include friction and wave drag. Their results for total resistance are shown in Figure 7-1.

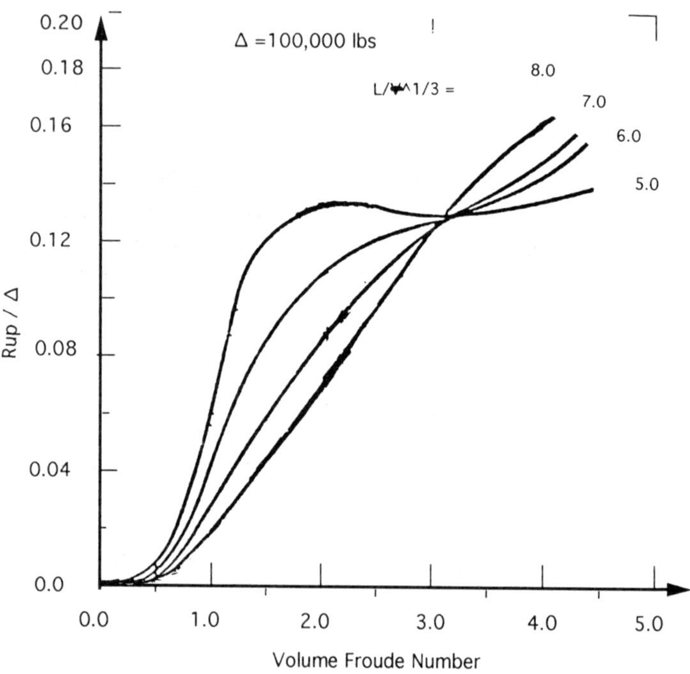


Figure 7-1
Upright Resistance for Fast Semi-Planing Hulls
(Savitsky and Gore, 1980)

The chart in Figure 7-1 is for a 100,000 pound displacement vessel. In order to convert this for use with other displacement vessels, it is recommended to use the following two relations

$$(R_{up}/\Delta)_{new} = (R_{up}/\Delta)_{100000} + ((C_{fricnew}\ (Rn) - C_{fric100000}\ (Rn)) + CA)$$
$$(1/2 \times W.S./\forall^{1/3}) \times F_\forall/\Delta\texttt{\^{}}2 \qquad (26)$$

where

$$C_{Fric} = 0.075 \div (\log Rn -2)\texttt{\^{}}2 \qquad (27)$$

per International Towing Tank Conference (ITTC)

$W.S./\forall^{2/3}$ = Wetted Surface of new vessel to Volume to the 2/3 power of the new vessel; it depends on the hull form and is often between 2 and 3

$CA$ = a correction factor for the new vessel sometimes taken as 0.0004 or zero

An example of another method of identifying the total resistance per pound displacement is to use the Measurement Handicap System (MHS) of Justin Kerwin (1978) with residuary coefficients of 1986. In that method, frictional resistance is often based on a 70% viscous length for the Reynolds number in the coefficient of friction estimate for displacement hull types for sailboats.

With $Rn$ as per Equation (27) and a vessel with a $L/\forall$ 1/3 ratio of 10 and a beam to draft ratio of 2, Table 7-1 coefficients apply. In Table 1 (from Kerwin (1978) with 1986 coefficients) these relationships also apply,

$$(R_{residuary}/\Delta) = a_1 \times (beam/draft)\texttt{\^{}}a_2 \times (C_\forall^2 \div \sqrt{(C\forall 2 + a_3)}) \times$$
$$(1 \div 10\texttt{\^{}}5) \qquad (28)$$

where

$$C_\forall = (10 \div (L/\forall^{1/3}))\texttt{\^{}}3$$

and per ITTC, $C_{Fric} = 0.075 \div (\log Rn -2)\texttt{\^{}}2 \qquad (27)$

| $R_T/\Delta$ | $R_{Fric}/\Delta$ | $R_{residury}/\Delta$ | $F_\nabla$ | $VB/\sqrt{L}$ | $a_1$ | $a_2$ | $a_3$ |
|---|---|---|---|---|---|---|---|
| .001074 | .0009241 | .00015 | .38 | .4 | 14.2 | .12 | 0.0 |
| .00253 | .00197 | .00056 | .57 | .6 | 49.4 | .19 | 0.0 |
| .00462 | .00331 | .00131 | .75 | .8 | 107.3 | .29 | 0.0 |
| .00796 | .00506 | .00290 | .94 | 1.0 | 241.9 | .26 | 0.0 |
| .0163 | .009315 | .00698 | 1.3 | 1.2 | 611.5 | .19 | 0.0 |
| .018 | .009587 | .00841 | 1.32 | 1.4 | 2,427.6 | .085 | 9.0 |
| .02319 | .01235 | .01084 | 1.51 | 1.6 | 7,421.8 | .046 | 49.0 |
| .0324 | .01527 | .01718 | 1.69 | 1.8 | 14,055.0 | .032 | 69.0 |
| .0465 | .01867 | .02788 | 1.88 | 2.0 | 25,500.0 | .020 | 85.0 |
| .0744 | .02238 | .05219 | 2.07 | 2.2 | 52,000.0 | .0125 | 100.0 |
| .0959 | .02641 | .06958 | 2.26 | 2.4 | 75,000.0 | .005 | 116.0 |

In table 1 use is made of these relationships as well.

$$C_V = (10 \div L/\nabla^{1/3})^3$$

$$F_\nabla = (VB/\sqrt{L}) \times (1/\sqrt{g}) \times \sqrt{(L/\nabla^{1/3})} \times 1.69$$

with $VB$ is knots, $L$ in feet and $g$ in feet per sec^2

and $(W.S. / \nabla^{2/3})$ is defined as $2.496 \times (L/\nabla^{1/3})^{1/2}$

# Table 7-1
## 1986 Measurement Handicap System (Kerwin, 1978), $C_v = 1$

The total resistance from Table 7-1 values for $C_v = 1$ are plotted in Figure 7-2.

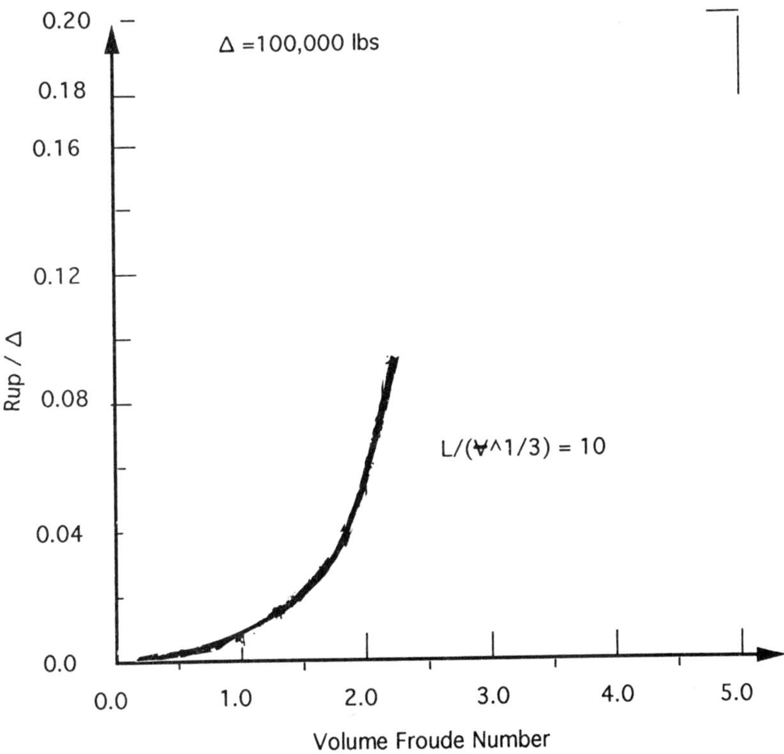


Figure 7-2
$R_{up}/\Delta$ versus $F_v$ Displacement Hull with
$L/\forall^{1/3} = 10$, $\Delta = 100,000$ lbs

These methods for estimating upright hull resistance have been provided for use with vessels to which the theory is applied. It is worth repeating that "one of the 'beauties' of the general theory presented here is that *RAWF* and *AWF* apply to however the resistance curve for a particular craft is estimated."

Next, a method for estimating appendage resistance will be presented.

Appendage Resistance

The keel and rudder surfaces are attached to the hull(s) of a sailboat to provide necessary course control for the vessel underway. When forces on these surfaces are activated by turning the rudder or turning the boat at flow angles of attack greater than zero, there is lift and accompanying induced drag resistance. There is also drag resistance from flow over the surfaces. This surface drag is present even when there is zero lift. This drag can be estimated as frictional drag using the total wetted surface with plan form area and a profile factor. It can also be estimated with frontal area and attached flow or separated flow coefficients. For estimating the appendage drag for vessel examples herein, appendage resistance is taken in a form that uses the frontal area as the reference area and this is defined as frontal area per pound displacement:

$$R_{app}/\Delta = C_d \, q_w \, (A_{ref}/\Delta) \tag{29}$$

where

$$C_{dattached} = 0.1$$
$$C_{dfully\ separated} = 1.0$$
$$q_w = 1/2 \, \rho w \, VB^2$$
$$A_{ref} = \text{frontal area of the appendage}$$
$$\rho_w = \text{density of water}$$
$$\Delta = \text{displacement of the vessel}$$

Appendage resistance for attached flow and fully separated flow with $A_{ref}/\Delta$ taken as 0.001 ft²/lb is presented in Figure 7-3.

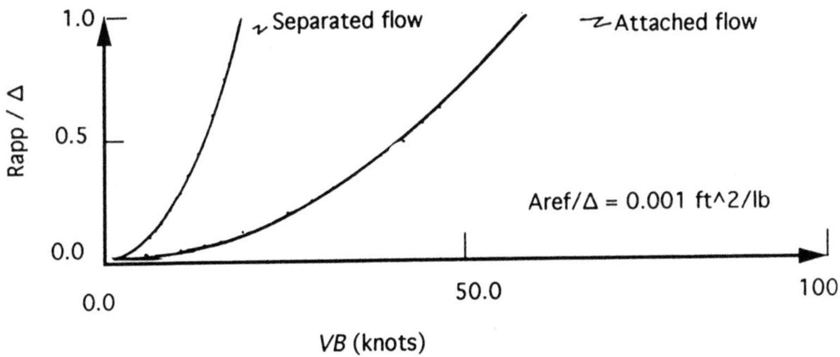


Figure 7-3
Appendage Resistance, Attached and Separated Flow,
$A_{ref}/\Delta$ = 0.001 ft$^2$/lb, $C_{d attached}$ = 0.1 and $C_{d fully\ separated}$ = 1.0

Fully attached flow occurs on efficient foil sections at leeway angles up to between 5° and 8°. At $\lambda = 25°$ it is fully separated. When $\lambda$ is known or estimated and is between 5° and 25°, a linear approximation for the drag coefficient can be made, assuming partially separated flow. This appendage resistance does not include induced drag resistance which is solely related to lift produced by the appendage and is already included in Available Wind Force of the LH side balance of driving force and resistance.

Heeled Resistance

Heeled resistance is generally taken as greater than zero for angles of heel greater than small. It can be estimated by comparing controlled towing tank experiment results for upright and heeled tows of model hulls. J. Gerritsma and J. A. Keunig (1989) provide a formula for two different models of the many models they have towed at Delft that includes a coefficient for induced drag resistance as well as one for added heeled resistance. Their expression corresponding to two models of Figure 7-4 is for an angle of heel in radians and is written as the difference between heeled and upright resistance.

$$\frac{(R_\phi - R_T)}{q_w\, S_c} = \frac{(C_o + C_2\, \phi^2)\, F_H^2}{q_w^2 \times S_c^2} + C_H \phi^2 \qquad (30)$$

where

$C_o$ is seen as an induced drag coefficient in addition to $C_H\phi\text{^}2$
$C_2$ is regarded as heeled drag coefficient
$C_H$ is the coefficient for the heeling force, $F_H$
$S_c$ is the wetted area for the hull, canoe body
$\phi$ is the angle of heel in radians

They provide a table for $C_o$ and $C_2$ and note, "The heeled resistance, which for the major part consists of induced resistance, differs approximately by a factor of two for equal side force at a heel angle of 20°" (p.15). Table 7-2 is for the body lines and specifications for the model geosims in Figure 7-4.

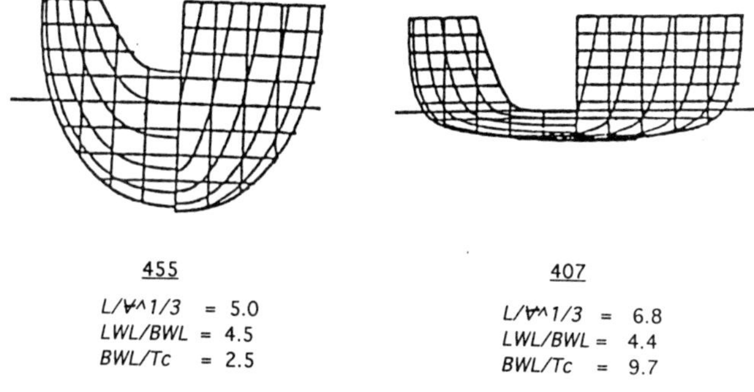


Figure 7-4

Body Plans of Models 407 and 455 (Gerritsma and Keunig, 1989)

| Model | $C_0$ | $C_2$ | $10^3\ C_H$ |
|---|---|---|---|
| Shallow draft 407 | 2.00 | 9.15 | 10.6 |
| Deeper draft 455 | 1.24 | 0.10 | 4.0 |

Table 7-2
Heeled Resistance Coefficients
(Gerritsma and Keunig, 1989, p.19)

An example of a specific upright resistance curve for a hull like
Gerritsma and Keunig's 407 is in Figure 7-5 and for a hull like
their 455 is in Figure 7-6. The scales have been changed to
reflect volume Froude number and $R/\Delta$ values. Those interested
further are encouraged to read the excellent paper by Gerritsma
and Keunig (1989).

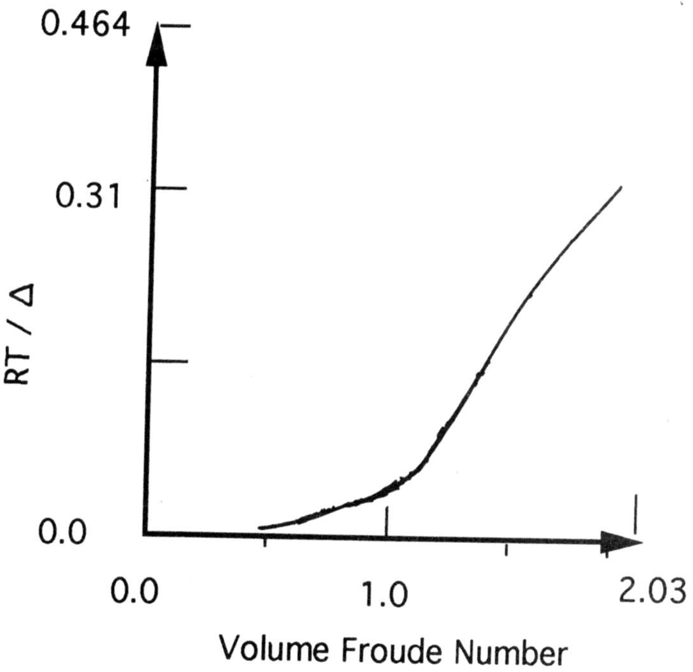


Figure 7-5
Upright Resistance for Hull 407 (Gerritsma and Keunig, 1989)

99

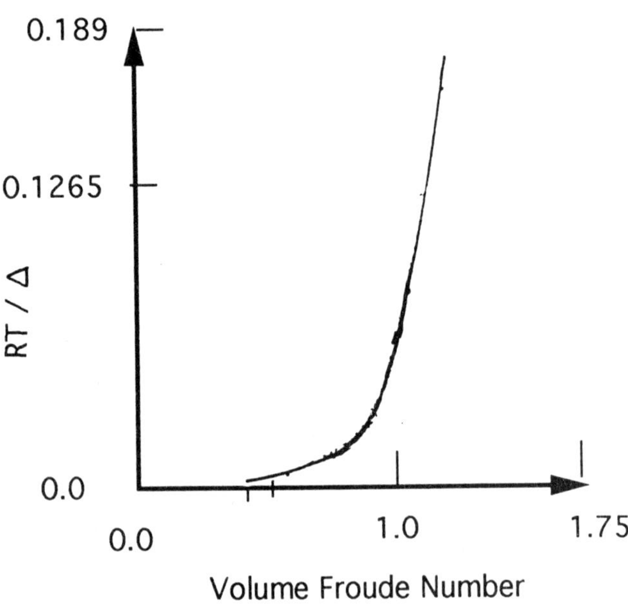



Figure 7-6
Upright Resistance for Hull 455 (Gerritsma and Keunig, 1989)

Heeled resistance, appendage drag (separated and attached), and upright hull resistance are all part of total resistance for Available Wind Forces and Raw Wind Forces in the general theory applications. The general theory applies to however total resistance per pound displacement is identified. The information is this chapter provides some simplified ways, compiled from the files of a simple-minded naval architect, so that total resistance can be estimated by users of the general theory for a broad range of sailboats.

There are many ways from acute past and present investigators to represent total resistance for forward motion of a sailboat hull. They all work for representing the RH side of the general theory when converted to resistance force pound per pound displacement.

The ways to estimate resistance in this chapter are for a broad range of sailboat hulls and appendage combinations. Those presented are not meant to replace fine-tuned tank estimates, or validated hydrodynamic flow code estimates on high-power computers in parallel for specific hull forms. However, the estimates based on the methods described here make quite accurate applications of the general theory possible for those users of the general theory who wish to condense specific sailboats to a point, $P_i$, and find equilibrium boat speeds from a specific moving point, $P_i$, with the theory or those who wish to start with a condensed point with character, find equilibrium speeds and then expand the point, $P_i$, found to actual sailboats in 3-D.

The next chapter provides example applications to two modern sailboats whose predicted speeds are close to actual speeds. Chapter 9 defines the limits of sailboat speed and Chapter 10 makes percent difference comparisons of predicted speeds and measured speeds for some known high-speed vessels.

# Chapter 8 - Two Examples of Applications to "Real Modern Sailboats," One Monohull and One Catamaran

This chapter presents two example applications of the general theory. One application is for a fast monohulled sailboat and the other is for a fast multihulled sailboat. Many sailmakers, racing sailors and naval architects will want to read it because the chapter is about practical applications. Other sailors will want to read it too, since the theory explains explicitly how a few crew on the rail effects the driving force for any sailboat. The general theory is applied to predict the speed of two specific high-performance sailboats by combining their Available Wind Force charts with their estimated resistance curves. This is done in regular winds for smooth water conditions for all true wind angles, $\Theta TW$. The resulting polar speed predictions are presented on true wind polar course charts.

Polar speed charts are representative of expected speeds for individual sailboats and are unique to each sailboat. On polar charts, speeds for the vessel are laid out graphically for each course angle. One course angle and one true wind speed plus the theory produces one equilibrium boat speed. Another course angle and the same true wind speed and the theory produces another equilibrium boat speed and so on. This process produces a polar-charted line of speed for the sailboat in the one true wind selected. What does a polar chart look like? Slice a red apple vertically through the core and look at the cross section. The biggest contour for the biggest wind on the polar chart is like the outer-skin edge contour of the split apple. The core contour line of the apple is for the slightest, most delicate breeze on the polar chart. From the general theory, such charts can be produced for any sailboat.

*Rowdy* is a medium-high performance monohull, owned and sailed by Mr. Charles Cheney. The polar chart for *Rowdy* produced from the general theory is shown as in Figure 8-1. To get a feel for the polar chart, run your finger around each contour for the "sailboat object" *Rowdy*.

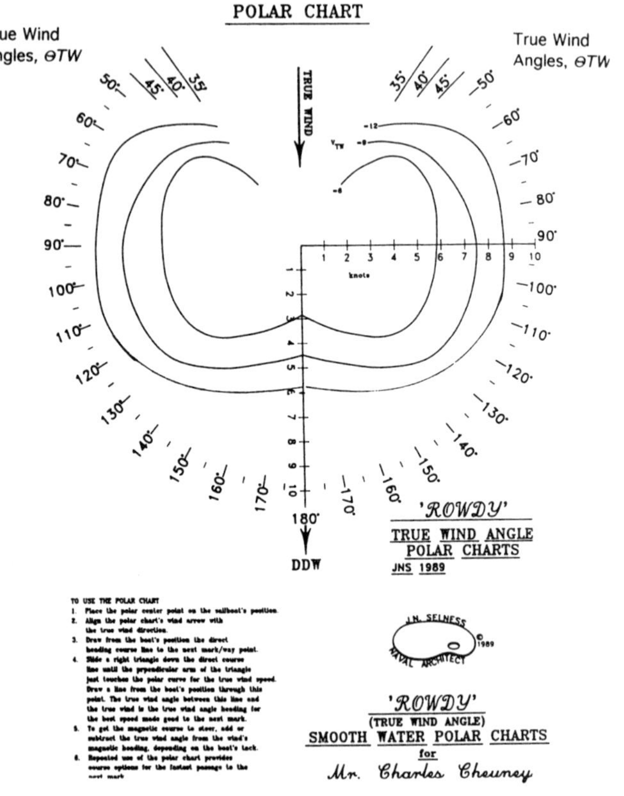


Figure 8-1
Polar Chart for *Rowdy*, a Monohull
at True Wind Angles, 35°- 180°

To produce these contours, which are unique to each sailboat, it is only necessary to have additional information: a drag-to-lift ratio versus apparent wind angle for the sails-rig, a coefficient-of-lift vs. apparent wind angle for the sails, and a righting moment curve for the hull or hulls plus an approximate resistance per pound displacement curve for the hull and a frontal area per pound displacement for the appendages. Specific information for sailboats comparable to *Rowdy* is in Table 8-1.

| | |
|---|---|
| $\Delta$ | 17,000 lbs |
| $\Delta$ with five crew | 18,000 lbs |
| *LWL* | 32.2 ft |
| *BWL* | 10.41 ft |
| *Hull Draft* | 1.83 ft |
| *W.S.* | ~250 ft^2 |
| *H* | 52.5 ft |
| *Keel Draft* | ~7.3 ft |

<u>A Rowdy Type Hull</u>

Table 8-1
Necessary Information for Use with the Theory
Estimated for *Rowdy*

For *Rowdy* the estimated required chart curves of $(C_D /C_L)$ versus
ß, $(C_L)$ versus ß, and *B/H* equivalent righting moment versus angle
of heel are shown in Figures 8-2, 8-3, and 8-4. A linear interpretation was used for estimating attached and separated flow drag on
the appendages with a frontal area to Δ ratio of 0.00142 ft²/lb.

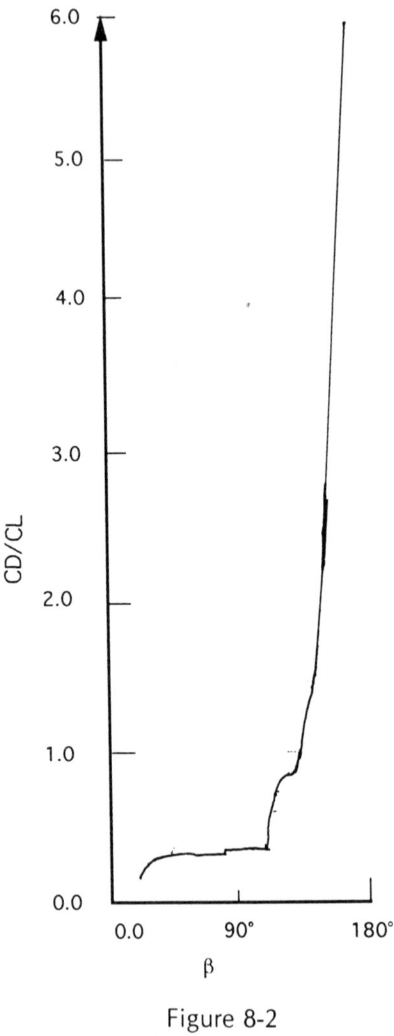


Figure 8-2
$(C_D /C_L)$ versus ß

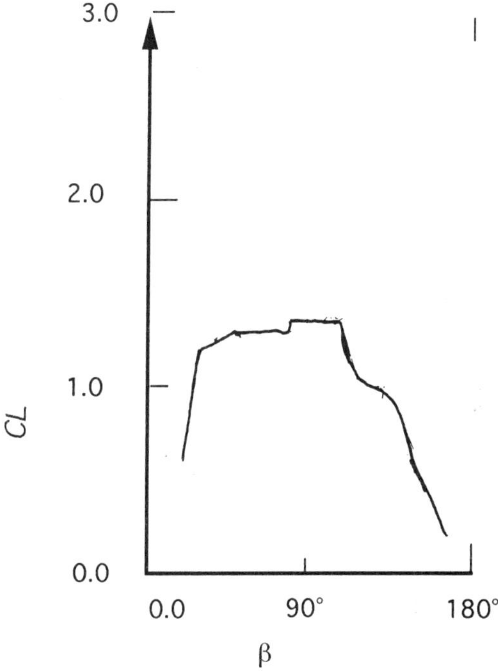


Figure 8-3
$(C_l)$ versus $\beta$

The assumed distribution of crew weight between those sitting on the rail getting the splash and those comfy in the cockpit can effect $(B/H)_{max}$. The effect of crew weight on the rail to Raw Wind Force driving forces is readily found from the theory as

$$(B/H)_{crew\ on\ the\ rail} = (B/H)_{all\ center\ cockpit}\ (1\ +\ \Delta_{crew\ rail}/\Delta_{total}) \quad (31)$$

This equation has been applied to the chart for *Rowdy* in Figure 8-4.

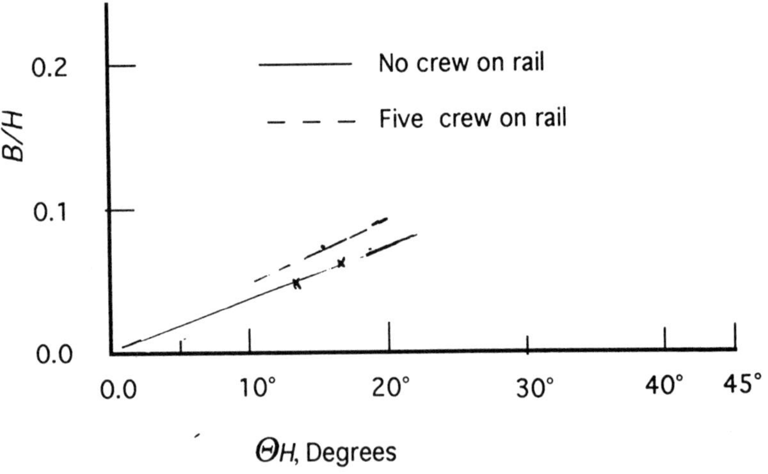


Figure 8-4
*B/H* versus Angle of Heel

Photo from
C. Cheyney

*Rowdy*

Sketch by JNS
from photo
by Gerri Conser
Costa Mesa, California

Distributions of live ballast (that is, crew weight) should be taken into account in predicting the top speed for a specific sailboat. The increase in *B/H* at less angle of heel is why, in *The Puzzle-master* (1991 manuscript) and *The Realm* (1996 manuscript) the character, Capt. Fang shouts, "To the rail ye hearties" (that is, ye hearties of the wind). He could easily have added, "Put your weight to work in the wind." Of course, what he means (should he think about it) in terms of the general theory is, "Increase *B/H* for the vessel's driving force, ye hearties."

The resistance curve for the hull as shown in Figure 8-5 is well established for this hull form and displacement and length. The general theory was applied at each $\theta TW$ to produce the predicted speeds of *Rowdy*'s polar chart. Run your finger around *Rowdy*'s polar chart curves in Figure 8-1.

Another example of a polar chart for a sailboat produced using the general theory is for *Cheshire Cat*, a 32-foot ocean-going CSK catamaran owned and sailed by Mr. Roger Grant. To produce this chart required estimating a resistance curve for conditions under sail. These conditions varied from sailing partly on one hull and partly on the other, to all on one hull at hull-afly speeds when the course and wind strength required that posture. Figure 8-6 illustrates the polar chart for *Cheshire Cat*. Run your finger around the outer contour of *Cheshire Cat's* polar chart.

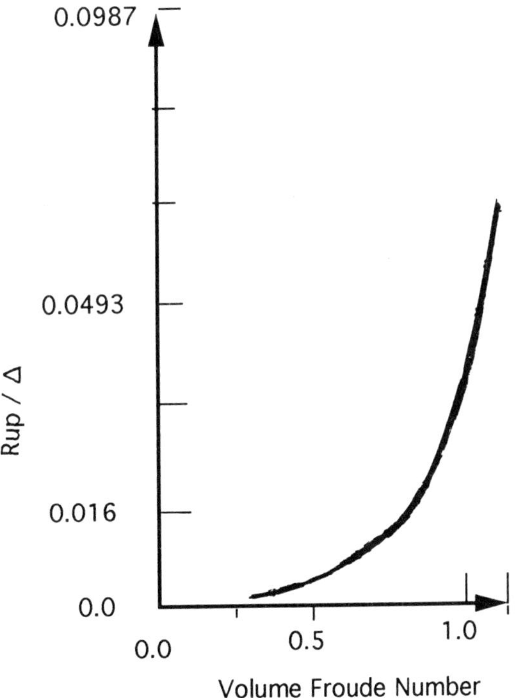


Figure 8-5
Resistance Curve for a Hull Like *Rowdy*'s
(Ref. Gerristma and Keunig)

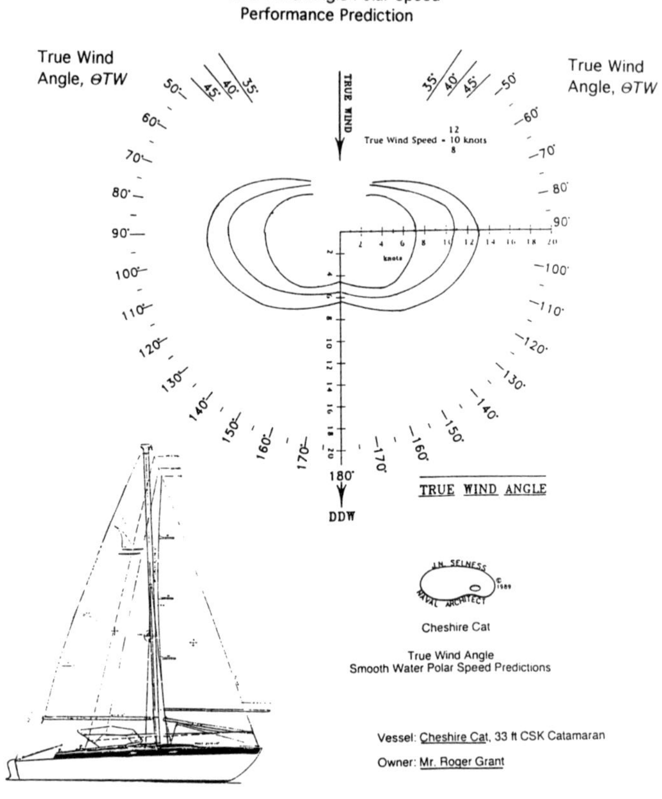


Figure 8-6
Polar Chart for *Cheshire Cat*, a Catamaran

*Chesire Cat's* polar chart is different from *Rowdy's*. In some winds and on some courses (wind abeam, $\ominus TW$ near 90°), *Cheshire Cat* can sail faster than the true wind speed.

These polar charts were produced by estimating information for the sails-rig in use, the actual hull and appendages, and assuming attached flow on the sails for $\beta < 90°$ and separated flow on the sails for $\beta > 110°$. The following relationships work with the general theory.

$B/H = 2 \; arm/H$

$$2 \; arm/H = 2 \, C_L \, [\cos \beta + (C_D/C_L) \sin \beta] \, q_a \, (S.A./\Delta) \, \mu \qquad (31)$$

The $(C_D/C_L)$ for the sails is a function of the apparent wind angle, $\beta$, estimated leeway angle, $\lambda$, and trim angle, $\delta$. George Hazen (1980) provides some possible estimated values of $C_D$ and $C_L$ versus $\beta$ for a variety of rigs. Sometimes $(C_D/C_L)$ is like that shown in Figure 8-7.

| | |
|---|---|
| $\Delta$ | 4,000 lbs |
| $\Delta$ with two crew | 4,400 lbs |
| *LOA* | 32.2 ft 3 inches |
| *LWL* | 27 ft 2 inches |
| *Beam Maximum* | 14 ft 6 inches |
| *Hull Draft* | 1 ft 4inches |
| *H* | 40 ft |
| *Draft* | |
| *(center board down)* | ~3 ft 10 inches |

Table 8-2
Necessary Information for Use with the Theory
Estimated for *Cheshire Cat*

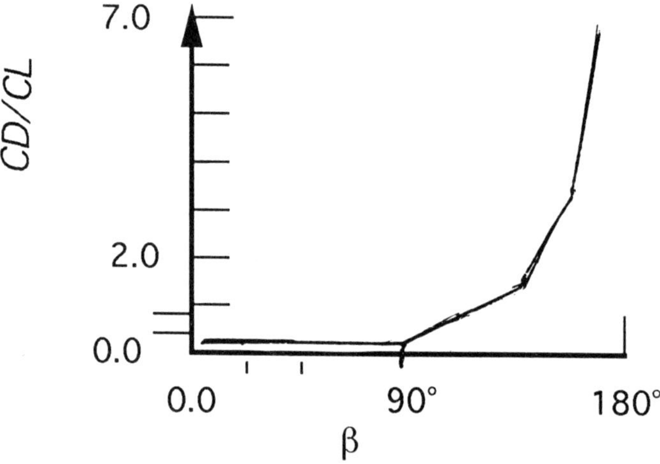



Figure 8-7
Typical $(C_D/C_L)$ versus ß

For these practical examples, $B/H$ is a function of $C_L$ and $\beta$ and $(C_D/C_L)$. The $(C_F/C_H)$ is a function of $(C_D/C_L)$ and $\beta$ and $\lambda$ and $\delta$. The fraction of mast height, $\mu$, is generally a constant, but can vary with the type of sails set. Generally, the range of $\mu$ is $0.4 < \mu < 0.6$ for all sailboats (interestingly, for some ancient vessels, $\mu$ was higher than 0.6; see Chapter 12).

Generally onboard any sailboat, the sail-rig is trimable to combinations of $C_D$ and $C_L$ or $C_L$ and $C_D/C_L$ equivalents that produce $C_F/C_H$ and $B/H$ for a given true wind angle course and wind strength and boat speed. Rapid increases of $B/H$ and $C_F/C_H$ with small changes in true wind course produce rapid increases in $RAWF$, and in turn produce the excitement of broaching—sudden accelerations along with out of control changes in course that wake the crew up on real-time sailboats underway and out at sea on a raucous, windy day. Equation (6) from Chapter 3 is given below.

$$RAWF = (B/H)\,(C_F/C_H)\,(1/2\mu) \qquad (6) \; *\!*\!*$$

The examples in this chapter serve to demonstrate the results of initial applications to monohulled and multihulled sailboats. The examples presented are but one way to use the theory. An alternate way of applying the theory is to assume a $(C_D/C_L)$ ratio for the sail-rig, select a $B/H$ ratio, then define $C_L$ with the condition that $C_L$ does not exceed a maximum for selected course angles and $S.A./\Delta$ ratios. This is done when $(B/H)_{max}$ is decided first for a class of vessels. From this preferred alternate view of deciding $(B/H)_{max}$ first, many possibilities for a class of sailboats can be explored before an actual sailboat is designed or built or the limits for sailboat speed can be defined.

This chapter has presented practical applications and the effect of crew weight on the rail. Proceeding with the preferred practical alternate view of the theory, the next chapter will define the exciting outer envelope limits for speeds of sailboats sailing a steady course in control.

Sketch by JNS

*Cheshire Cat*

Photo by JNS

116

# Chapter 9 - The Limits for Sailboat Speed

This chapter presents limits for speeds for sailboats sailing straight true wind courses, under control, on smooth waters in true wind speeds of from 5 knots to 100 knots. That limits to sailboat speed do exist is evident from the general theory results of Chapters 3 and 5. That limit speeds for sailboats do exist has not always been clear from past theories or they have been found to be extremely large (Smith 1989). This chapter, therefore, in establishing intersecting envelope boundaries that determine the limits of sailboat speed, advances the understanding of the sailboat.

The limits of sailboat speed occur naturally from a general theory application as the solution to a minimal-maximal problem. The LH side, the driving force side, of Equation (13) is maximized and the RH side, the resistance side, of (13) is minimized. Available Wind Force is maximized while Total Resistance (for available wind force) is minimized to produce sets of maximum possible speeds for the sailboat.

Available Wind Force = Total Resistance

Translation in direction of motion, $VB$

$$\eta F_{adf} - F_{windage} - F_{indkeel} = F_{wrf} \quad (13)$$

The LH side of (13) is maximized by maximizing $B/H$ and $C_F/C_H$ for all true wind courses and speeds, while $\mu$ is set at 0.4, a supportable minimum for maximization. Windage and induced drag resistance are also minimized for maximization of Available Wind Force. The condition of maximization of the LH side, for high-speed vessels and for all true wind courses, requires a true wind course between 90° and 143°. Generally for a high-speed vessel, at speed, the apparent wind angle, $\beta$, is less than 25°, thus the lowest possible drag to lift ratio maximizes the LH side, as can be seen from Figure 9-1 where Raw Wind Forces ($RAWF$) versus sail-rig drag to lift ratios($C_D/C_L$) for select apparent wind angles ($\beta$) < 90° are plotted with $B/H$ = 0.8, and $\mu$ = 0.4.

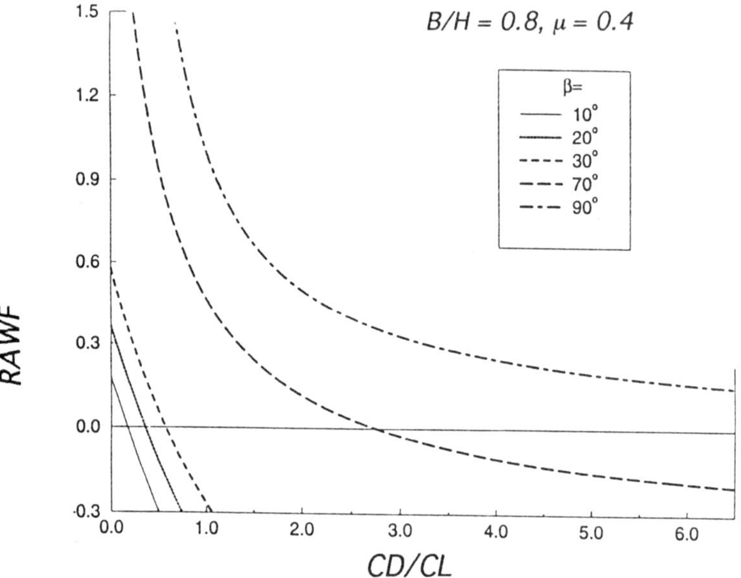


Figure 9-1
*RAWF* Versus $C_D/C_L$ for ß < 90°

The *B/H* ratio at which a sailboat can sail, in a practical way for any period of time, is dependent on the structural load-carrying capabilities of the craft, as well as the righting characteristics of the craft. Current high-speed blue-water craft (such as *Aikane* and *Enza*) sail at *B/H* < 0.8. Other specialized record-setting, speed-burner craft sail at a *B/H* < 2.4. (See Chapter 10 where attained real speeds and predicted speeds are compared for specific speed-burner craft of recent history.) Most sailing vessels today sail at a *B/H* much less than 0.8. Yet it is the limits of sailboat speed that is considered here, so *B/H* is set equal to 0.8, a high value, for winds up to 100 knots. Limit speeds for craft with *B/H* = 1.6 and 2.4 are also found for winds up to 50 knots, corresponding to a Beaufort scale of 11 (Marcaj 1964). A drag to lift ratio of 0.15 is selected to represent the Available Wind Force for a limit boat that sails at limit speeds. This represents an efficient rig as found from wind tunnel tests on sails, as illustrated in Figure 9-2. The sail-rig is efficient in that there is a range of $\Omega$ for which the drag to lift ratio is small. When flow separation on the sails begins to occur just after maximum $C_L$, then the rig efficiency is less for most points of sail and boat speed. For more sail-rig test data see for example Marchaj (1979) or Norwood (1979).

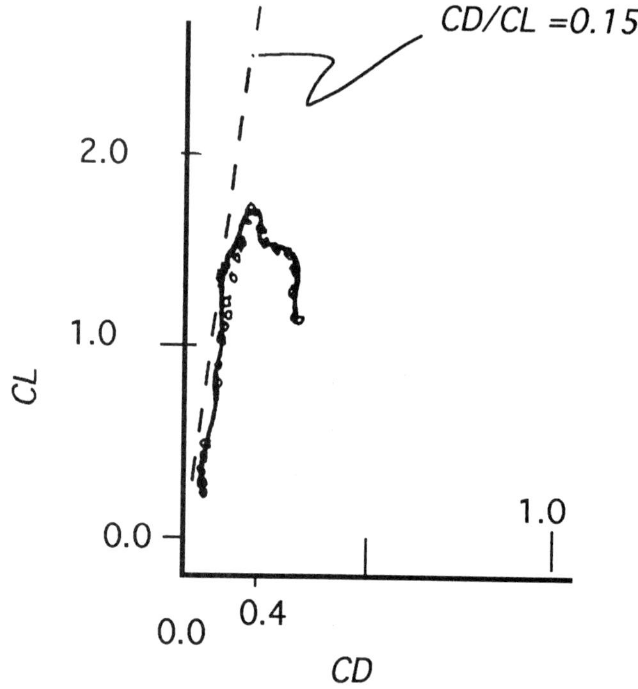



Figure 9-2
Wind Tunnel Test Results on an Efficient Rig (Otto Scherrer 1974)
$\Omega = 0°$ to $26°$, Max $C_L$ at $\Omega = 20°$

The points on each line in Figure 9-5  that represent limit speeds were produced by applying to maximized driving force curves of the theory an estimated minimum resistance curve that represents a minimum resistance at each speed for a minimum resistance vessel for that speed. The minimum resistance curve used for the upright hull is given in Figure 9-3 for a displacement of 8000 pounds. It is taken from the lowest resistance parts of Figures 7-1 and 7-2.

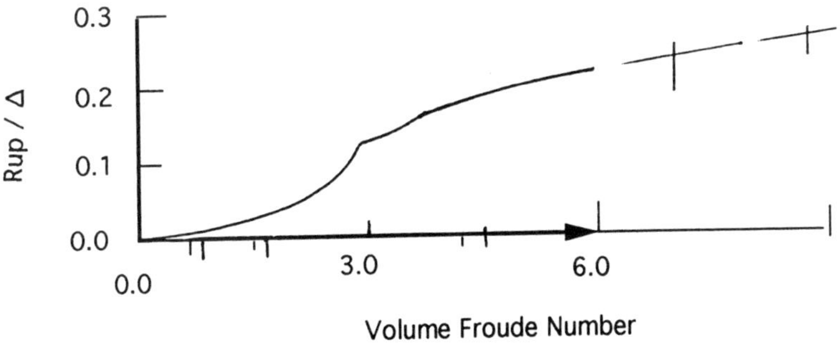


Figure 9-3
Minimum Upright Hull Resistance Curve

Figure 9-3 is not a resistance curve for any specific boat but is a composite curve of estimated minimums at each speed to obtain total resistance at each speed for all hulls, displacement and planing. Added to this basic hull resistance at each speed is either appendage drag for attached flow, or appendage drag for separated flow. The appendage drags are from Figure 7-3. Thus minimum total resistance is defined by three curves, one for attached flow on the appendages, one for separated flow on the append-ages, and one from Figure 9-3 for minimum upright hull resistance. That Figure 9-3 is a very good estimate of upright hull resistance for limit boats is attested to by a comparison with recent minimum hull resistances for a double-ended Wigley hull (it has a sharp point at both ends), calculated by Alexander H. Day and Lawerence J. Doctors (1997) using frictional and wave resistance theories for a displacement hull of 22,600 pounds. Day and Doctors' data points are plotted on Figure 9-4 with x marks along with the curve of Figure 9-3. The agreement, by inspection, is very good.

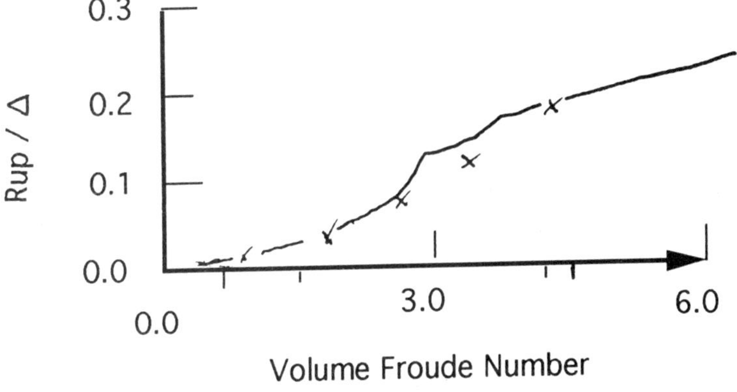

Figure 9-4
Minimum Upright Hull Resistance (X) for a Wigley Hull
(Day and Doctors 1997)
and Minimum Upright Hull Resistance Curve from Figure 9-3

For total minimum resistance, heeled resistance is set equal to zero. Separated flow drag on the hull is also set equal to zero. Thus upright resistance plus attached flow resistance on the appendages is the minimum resistance, $\underline{R}_{Tmin}$, that combines with the maximum driving forces to form the upper bound on the limits to sailboat speed. These limits are defined by the intersection of the minimum resistance curve with the appropriate maximum Available Wind Force curve for each true wind speed. A lower bound to limit speeds is provided by defining the minimum resistance as upright resistance plus separated flow resistance on the appendages. So in symbol form, the bounds on resistance are

$$\underline{R}_{Tmin} > R_{up} + R_{appatt}$$

or

$$R_{Tmin} < R_{up} + R_{appsep}$$

With these resistance conditions and the driving force conditions set for $B/H$, $C_D/C_L$ and $\mu$, for limit boats performance, the upper bound limits for sailboat speed can be found and are shown in Figure 9-5 for attached flow on the appendages and at $B/H$ ratios of 0.08, 1.6, and 2.4. The lower bound limit can also be found and is shown for separated flow on the appendages and a $B/H$ of 0.8. In Figure 9-5 the true wind speed is read from the horizontal axis and the limit speeds are read from the vertical axis. For example, at a true wind speed of 50 knots, the limit for $B/H = 0.8$ and attached appendage flow is 58 knots. For another example, at a true wind speed of 30 knots, $B/H = 0.8$ and separated appendage flow, the limit is 28 knots.

# The Limits for Sailboat Speed

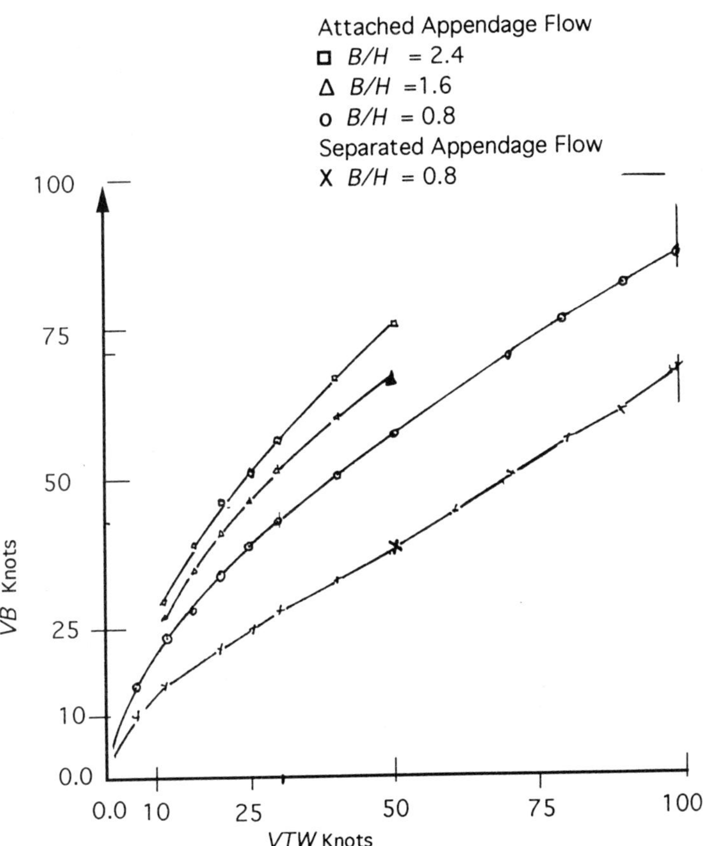



Figure 9-5
The Limits for Sailboat Speed

Each sailboat speed point on the limit speed curves in Figure 9-5 corresponds to one true wind speed on the true wind axis. Each curve corresponds to a set *B/H* of the curve value, an available wind curve for that true wind speed, and true wind courses between 90° and 143° plus a minimum resistance curve. Figure 9-6 gives an example of the determination of a single point on a curve of Figure 9-5. The intersect of the driving force curve (*AWF*) and the minimum total resistance curve is the limit speed for the true wind speed of 30 knots and *B/H* = 0.8. That speed is 43 knots. (Intersects with *AWF* for *B/H* = 1.6 and 2.4 produce higher limit speeds.)

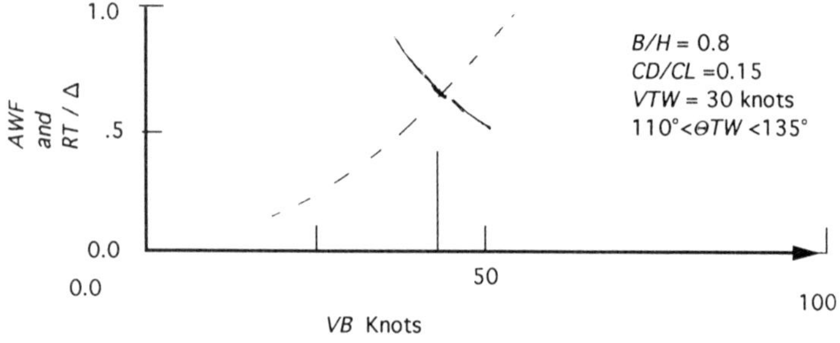


Figure 9-6
One Point of a Limit to Sailboat Speed Curve,
*AWF/Δ* for One *VTW*

126

The results in Figure 9-5 show that there are limits to controlled sailboat speed on smooth waters no matter what the wind speed. Even for 100 knots of wind the theory limit is 90 knots for $B/H$ = 0.8 and smooth waters.

What do other authors say about the limits of sailboat speed? There are only a few authors who have stuck their necks out and said there are limits. C.A. Marchaj, on page 86 of his monumental *Aerodynamic and Hydrodynamics* (1979), says, "By ballasting the windward hull (sandbagging to the maximum) an almost unlimited righting moment can be provided. Speed is practically restricted only by the strength of the hull's structure and of rigging, and of course the state of the sea." John Letcher, on page 141 of his theory (1976) says of his theory, "Present analysis provides an upper bound on performance for ideal limiting cases where the harmful effects of heeling, wave resistance and sail area are completely avoided." (See annotated bibliography.) Bernard Smith, in his delightful book *Sailloons and Fliptackers* (1989), sides with Marchaj and uses a hypothesized efficiency model for the hulls, appendages, and sails to define a set of limits that are very, very large. Smith's model of limit speeds deserves a close look.

Smith's model of sailboat speed limits rests on a combination of two drag angles, one for the sails and another for the hull, plus the apparent wind angle. All are combined via the apparent wind speed line of the velocity wind triangle, essentially combining Equations (1) and (2) into one balance while ignoring righting moment developed and required for each speed. Figure 9-7 presents a proof of this drag angle law (see figure for law)) for upright sailboats (after Marchaj 1964).

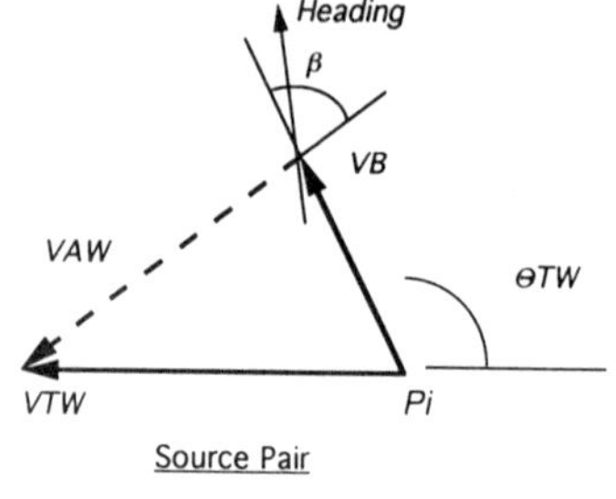


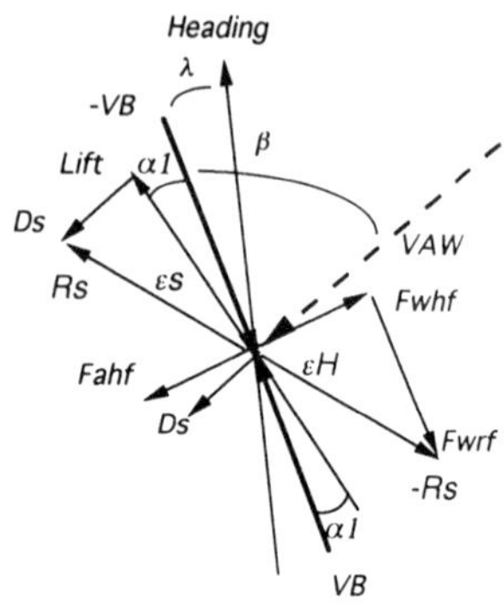


All the action is located at *Pi*

$$\beta + \alpha1 = 90°$$

$$\varepsilon H + \varepsilon S + \alpha1 = 90°$$

$$\beta - \varepsilon H - \varepsilon S = 0°$$

$$\beta = \varepsilon H + \varepsilon S$$

Proof of Drag Angle Law
With Source Pair

# Figure 9-7
## All the Angles and the Drag Angle Result
## at Hypothesized Equilibrium Speed

Other theorists, notably aerodynamist Marchaj (1964), Princeton Mathematician H.C. Curtiss (1976), and Physicist Norwood (1979), have seized on this angle relation to form theories. That this significant relationship of drag angles and ß exists is possibly attributed first to Lancaster in 1907 (Marchaj 1979). It is repeated in Marchaj (1964) and is used by most sailboat theorists today. It provides a good check on any performance predictions for specific sailboats for any theory. In the general theory of this treatise, it is automatically satisfied at equilibrium speed.

Marchaj (1979), using the drag angle relationship as a theory, speaks of the 10° sailboat (that is, the drag angle for the sails plus the drag angle for the hull and keel equals 10°). Smith (1989) puts bounds on the drag angles and apparent wind angles with a 14° sailboat with hypothetical sails and keel to produce a set of limit ratios for each true wind heading, the maximum of which is first found for 13.4 knots of *VTW*. Then he argues (p. 60) that the same ratio applies in proportion to the ratios of squares of all wind speeds to the square of 13.4 knots regardless of heeling and righting moments. Smith's big set of limit speeds is charted and compared to one set of limit speed results ($B/H = 0.8$) from the general theory in Figure 9-8.

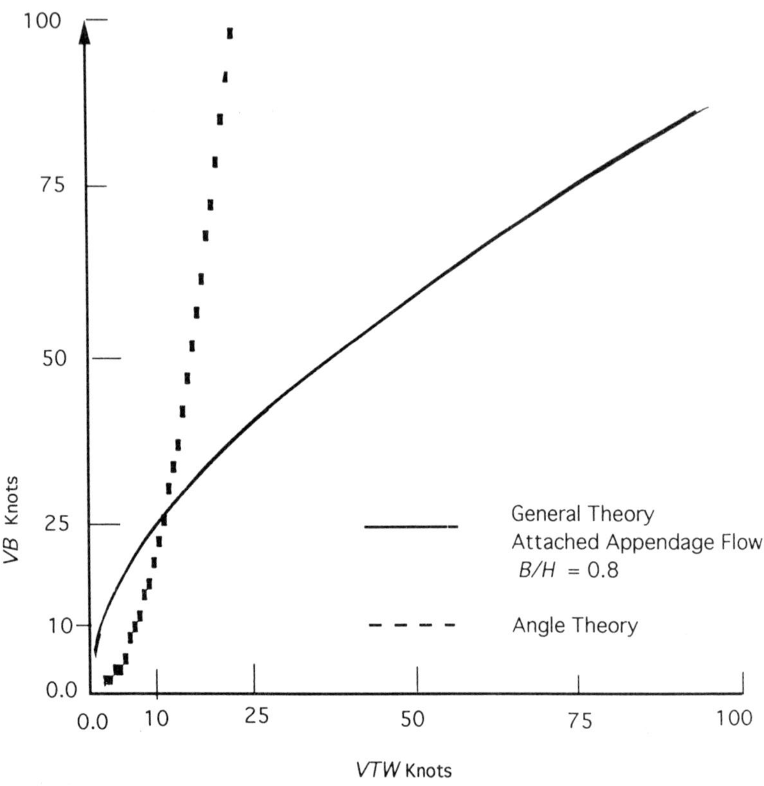


Figure 9-8
B.Smith's Angle Theory Limits of Sailboat Speed Compared with
the General Theory Limits of Sailboat Speed (Defined Herein)

130

It is clear from this comparison that righting moments included in the general theory produce a divergent result from Smith's "drag angle law" application. A different set of limit speeds for the sailboat object of nature is produced by the general theory than that produced by theories that do not include righting moment.

One of the head-shaking features of the general theory results is that they incorporate righting moment, drag to lift ratios of sails-rigs (sensitive to leeway angle, $\lambda$), and the apparent wind angle of the velocity triangle, all into a single expression that represents the driving force of the sailboat in Equation (8). When 0.8 is selected as representing a maximum $B/H$ for current blue-water vessels and $\mu$ is selected as 0.4 (a supportable close estimate of a minimum for $\mu$), and $\lambda$ is small such that $C_D/C_L$ is a set related to $\beta$ remains true, then Equation (8) of Chapter 3 becomes

$$(B/H)\ (C_F/C_H)\ (1/2\mu)\ =$$

$$(B/H)\ \frac{[\sin(\beta) - (C_D/C_L)\cos(\beta)]}{[\cos(\beta) + (C_D/C_L)\sin(\beta)]}\ (1/2\mu) \qquad (8) \quad ****$$

$$(0.8)\ \frac{[\sin\beta - (C_D/C_L)\cos\beta]}{[\cos\beta + (C_D/C_L)\sin\beta]}\ (1/0.8) \qquad (9)$$

Equation (8) or (9) can be used in the Available Wind Force equation for translation in direction of motion, $VB$, Equation (13).

$$\eta\ F_{adf} - F_{windage} - F_{indkeel} = \underline{F}_{wrf} \qquad (13)$$

Further, if $(C_D/C_L)$ is set at 0.15 from empirical test results on rigs, then Equation (9), which is part of the LH side of Equation (13) and all of the LH side of (4), defines the boundary of speed possibilities for all bluewater sailboats capable of sailing at $B/H = 0.8$ on smooth waters! When smooth-water resistance of the RH side of (4) is less than or equal to its rough water resistance then the limits are as shown in Figure 9-5. Anything that decreases the minimum of the RH side will increase the limit boundary. Anything that increases the maximum of the LH side will increase the limits. Thus the limits presented are a best estimate for smooth waters. How good these estimates are is discussed in the next chapter.

Why use this general theory rather than some computed algorithm that runs on a supercomputer for 24 hours and then produces sailboat speed predictions? Simply this: the general theory shows that the sailboat object is not as simple as some theories would make it, nor is it as complex as others would make it. Most of all, the general theory provides understanding that sailboat speed is an identifiable-determinate process!

In this chapter an approximation to the limit speeds for sailboats under control on smooth waters has been presented. These fundamental results have been compared in a startling comparison with the recent results from another theorist. The next chapter will predict speeds for specific high-speed craft using the general theory, and then the predicted speeds will be compared with the officially recorded speeds of each craft. That comparison is made with a continuation of the philosophy that the general theory is a fundamental theory to be proven out with time and use, use and time.

# Chapter 10 - Comparison of General Theory
# Predictions with Experimental Results

This chapter examines the important question, "How well do predictions of sailboat speed from the general theory compare with the 'reality' of experiments with real sailboats?" It is a scientific question all theories regarding the workings of an object of nature must face. To answer this question it is necessary to have: 1) accurate, measured speeds for a specific craft with the true wind speed it sails in, and 2) predicted sailing speeds from the theory.

Predictions with the theory can only be made when given enough data about a vessel to estimate its $B/H$ at speed and to estimate a $C_D/C_L$ ratio for the sail-rig combo, and enough hull information to estimate a resistance curve for the vessel at speed. In short, it could require a major testing program costing hundreds of thousands of dollars to make this experimental-scientific comparison. This was out of the question for the author to undertake. Fortunately, the speeds of several high-speed sailboats have been recorded accurately under the auspices of the World Sailing Speed Record Council (IYRU/WSSRC) guidelines and reported by the IYRU/World Sailing Speed Record Council (1995/97). These same vessels have been described sufficiently in other publications to gather enough information about the vessels for producing $B/H$ and resistance estimates for them and make reasonable speed predictions using the theory.

The names of the vessels compared with their relevant data and reference sources numbered are listed in Table 10-1. The special references for the vessels used in this comparison are listed at the end of this chapter. An estimated sailing $B/H$ is produced from an analysis of information in these references. Other references germane to the general theory are listed in the bibliography at the end of this treatise. Additional references for the interested reader are further listed in the annotated bibliography after the appendices.

| Vessel | Type Vessel | Length (ft) | Beam (ft) | Δ (lbs) with crew | Mast H (ft) | B/H (est.) |
|---|---|---|---|---|---|---|
| Yellow-Pages Endeavor (7,4,3,8) | Proa-Pod | (not known) | 50 | 680 | 39 | 2.0 |
| Bielak Sailboard (3) | Sailboard | ~8 | ~2 | 250 | 15+ | 4 |
| Longshot (2,6,3) | Tri-foil Hydrofoil | 18 | 18 | ~400 | 15.5 | 2.0 |
| Crossbow II (1,5,3) | Semi-proa | 60 | 24.75 | 5000 | 60 | .51 |
| Crossbow (1,5,3) | Proa | 60 | 28 | 3800 | 60 | .38 |

| Vessel | Total Resistance For Prediction |
|---|---|
| Yellow Pages Endeavor | tan 4° + $R_{appatt}$ (Chapter 7) |
| Bielok Sailboard | Limit Boat Resistance (Chapter 9) |
| Longshot | .08 + $R_{appatt}$ (Chapter 7) |
| Crossbow II | Limit Boat Resistance (Chapter 9) |
| Crossbow | Limit Boat Resistance (Chapter 9) |

Table 10-1. High-Speed Sailing Vessels (Ref. number in parenthesis)

## Table 10-1
## High-Speed Sailing Vessels

*Yellow Pages-Endeavor* (the current record holder), *Bielak Sail-board*, *Longshot*, *Crossbow II*, and *Crossbow* are the names of the vessels whose speeds are compared with theory. *Yellow Pages-Endeavor*, sailed by Simon McKeon of Australia, is a three-hull proa-pod craft designed by Lindsay Cunningham. The *Bielak Sailboard*, sailed by Thierry Bielak, is a sailboard. *Longshot*, sailed by Russell Long, is a trifoil hydrofoil designed by Greg Ketterman. *Crossbow II*, sailed by Tim Coleman, is a bi-sail semi-proa of staggered hulls designed by Macalpine-Downie. *Crossbow*, sailed by Tim Coleman and T. Hall, is a proa. These are the boats whose actual speeds are compared to predicted speeds from the general theory. Example calculations for $B/H$ of each vessel are in Figure 10-1.

$$\Delta_T = W_{board} + W_{sailor}$$

$$\text{Righting Moment} \approx \ell_1 W_{board} + \ell_2 W_{sailor}$$

$$W_{board} \approx 50 \text{ lbs}$$
$$W_{sailor} \approx 200 \text{ lbs}$$
$$\ell_1 \approx 1 \text{ ft}$$
$$\ell_2 \approx 3.5 \text{ ft}$$

$$arm_{max} = \frac{1 \times 50 + 3.5 \times 200}{50 + 200} = \frac{750}{250}$$

$$\left(\frac{2\,arm_i}{H}\right)_{max} = \frac{2 \times \frac{750}{250}}{15} = .4 = \left(\frac{B}{H}\right)_{equivalent\ max}$$

assume record run at near $\left(\frac{B}{H}\right)_{equivalent\ max}$, set $\left(\frac{B}{H}\right) = .4$ for estimat

## A. *Bielok Sailboard*

Figure 10-1<br>
Calculations for *B/H* Estimates for Each Vessel

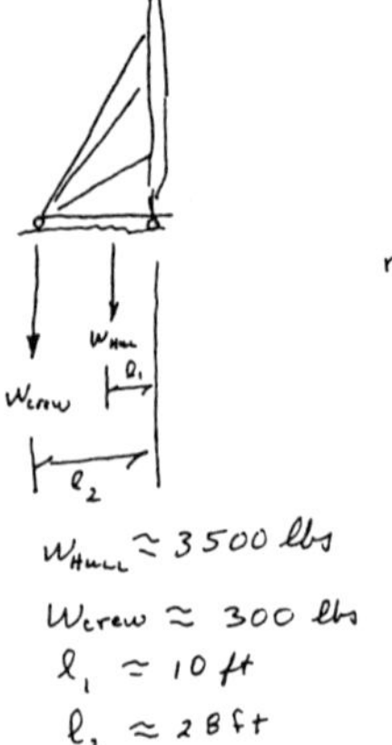



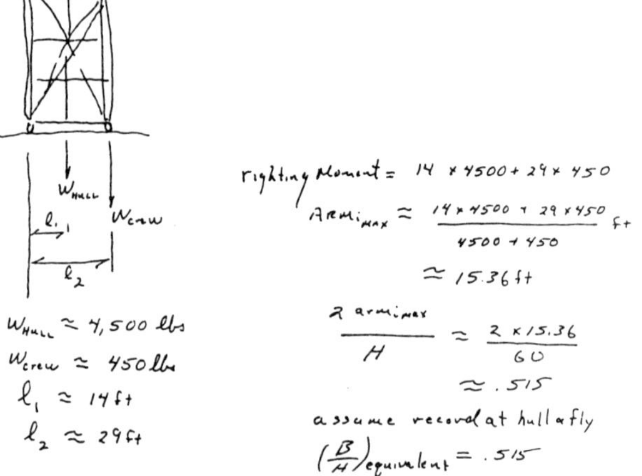

$$\text{righting Moment} \approx 28 \times 300 + 10 \times 3500$$

$$arm_{max} \approx \frac{28 \times 300 + 10 \times 3500}{(300 + 3500)}\ ft$$

$$\approx 11.42\ ft$$

$$\frac{2\ arm_i}{H} = \frac{2 \times 11.42}{60} \approx .38$$

assume record at PROA POS A fly

$$\left(\frac{B}{H}\right)_{estimate} = .38$$

## B.  *Crossbow*



$$\text{righting Moment} = 14 \times 4500 + 29 \times 450$$

$$ARM_{i\ MAX} \approx \frac{14 \times 4500 + 29 \times 450}{4500 + 450}\ ft$$

$$\approx 15.36\ ft$$

$$\frac{2\ arm_{i\ MAX}}{H} \approx \frac{2 \times 15.36}{60}$$

$$\approx .515$$

assume record at hull a fly

$$\left(\frac{B}{H}\right)_{equivalent} = .515$$

## C.  *Crossbow II*

Figure 10-1, continued
Calculations for *B/H* Estimates for Each Vessel

An example calculation of predicted speed for *Yellow Pages-Endeavor* is in Figure 10-2. The predicted and achieved speeds for the variety of high speed sailboats are compared in Figure 10-3 and Table 10-2.

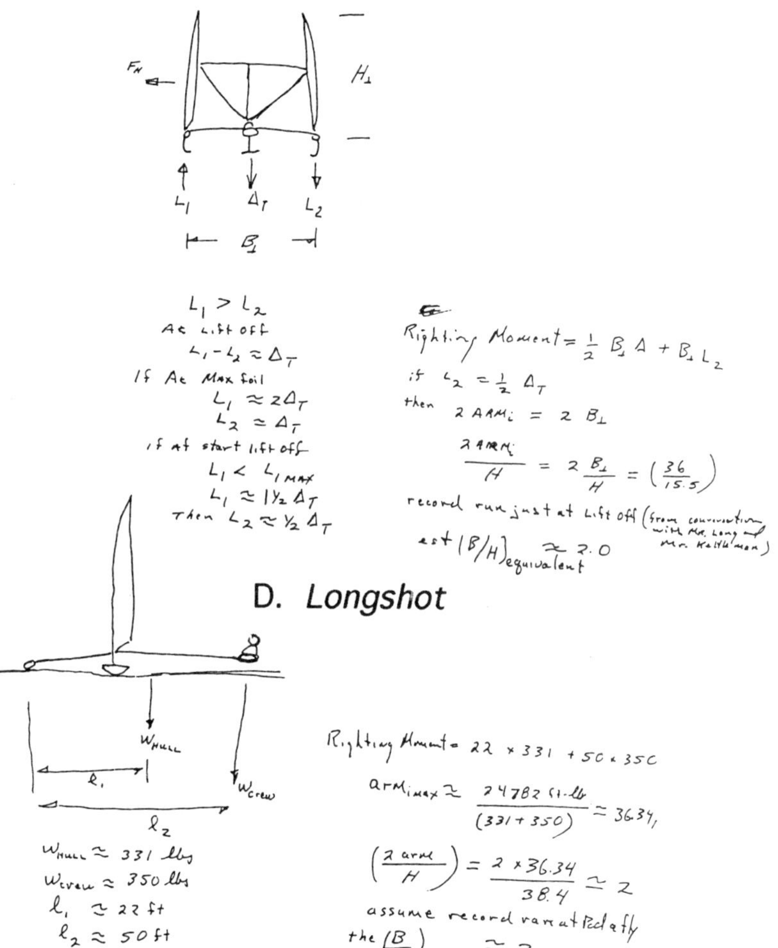


Figure 10-1, continued

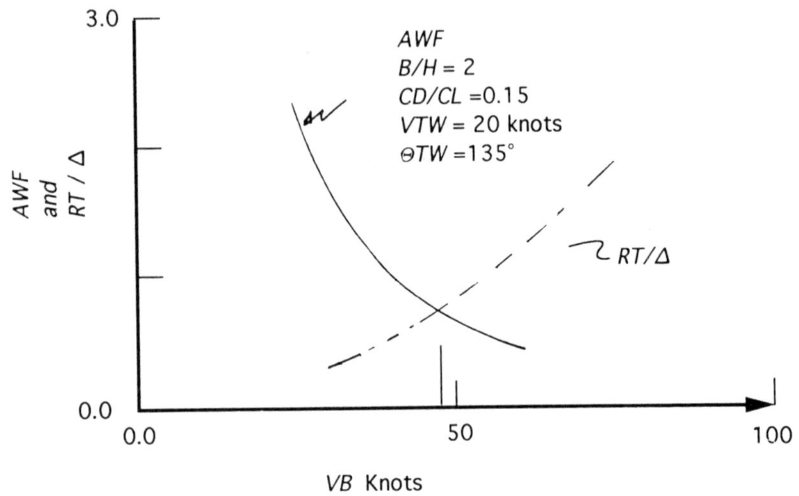



Figure 10-2
Example Calculation of Predicted Speed
for *Yellow Pages-Endeavor*

| Vessel (year) | WSSA Recorded | Est. True Wind | General Theory Predicted | % difference |
|---|---|---|---|---|
| | (knots) | (knots) | (knots) | % |
| Yellow-Pages Endeavor (1993) | 46.52 | 20 | 47 | 1 |
| Bielak Sailboard (1993) | 45.32 | 50 | 48 | 6 |
| Longshot (1992) | 43.6 | 20 | 46 | 6 |
| Crossbow II (1980) | 36 | 27 | 34 | 6 |
| Crossbow (1973) | 29.3 | 20 | 25 | 15 |

Table 10-2
Recorded and Predicted Speeds

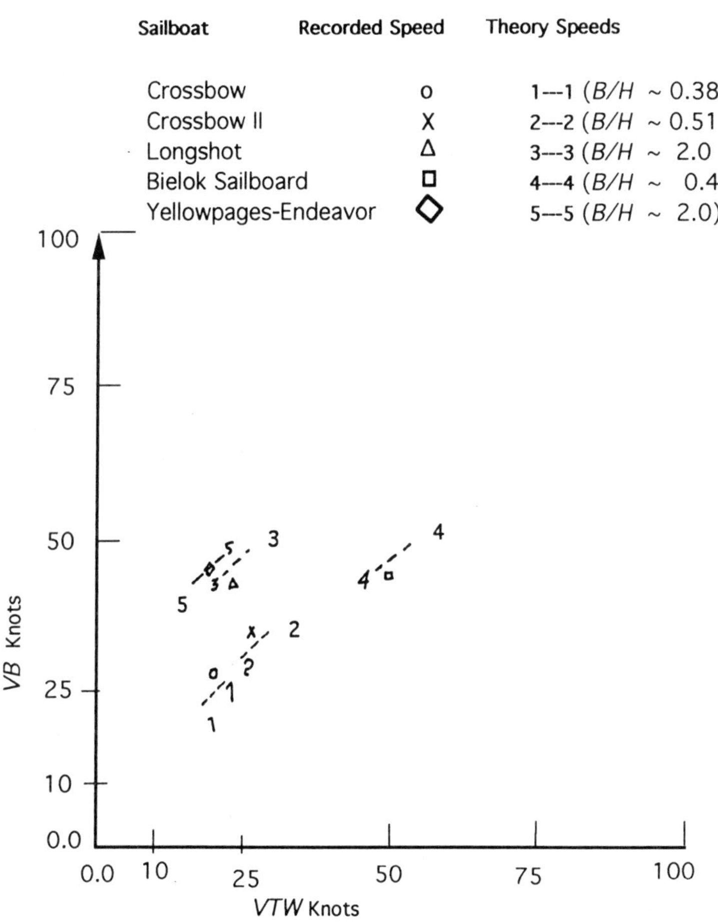


Figure 10-3
Record Speeds and Predicted Speeds Compared for
WSSRC Vessels

139

The percentage difference in Table 10-2 is defined as the difference between the WSSRC speed and the predicted speed divided by WSSRC speed, then that quantity times 100.

$$\% \text{ difference} = ((\text{WSSRC} - \text{predicted}) \div \text{WSSRC})) \times 100$$

The percentage difference between speed recorded and speed predicted is between 1% and 15%. Therefore, comparison between predicted results of the general theory and actual on-the-water results tends to validate and provide efficacy to the theory.

It is the general perception that a comparison with controlled experimental results implies a validation of a theory. Such a validation appears to exist. However, this theory works because it has to. That is to say, it is close enough to the reality to mirror the reality so it has to. Being theory it can open up, with time and use, new avenues of understanding and application regarding the phenomena, the sailboat object, wherever that object be.

The different kinds of craft in the applications in Chapters 8-12 show that the general theory for the sailboat applies to a wide range of sailing craft.

In summary, this treatise on the general theory for the sailboat has broken new ground. The performance of actual sailboats has been compared with predictions based on the theory and has brought efficacy to the theory. Predicted speeds in the form of polar charts for a monohull and a multihull have been presented. The form and shape of the envelope limits of sailboat speed have been found. Ways to estimate resistance for use with the general theory have been provided. Raw Wind Forces from a mathematical primitive expression of the general theory have been modified to Available Wind Forces to make even clearer how nature works with the sailboat. Chapter 3 presented the free modulating function method of solution that produces the general theory and its core result. The core result is a primitive mathematical expression that represents the driving forces for the sailboat that includes righting moment characteristics of a sailboat. Chapter 2 contains a description of all the angles for an upright sailboat on smooth waters. Together with its definitions and tautologies, it set up the general theory of Chapter 3. A blank page like that in the addendum, plus perspiration, and then inspiration brought the general theory and its advances in the understanding of the sailboat. The reader is encouraged to mark in the margins of the text and write on the blank page of the addendum.

The theory, while wrought from thinking about the sailboat as an object of nature, is general. Being general, it can be applied wherever and whenever the assumptions made to form the theory can be applied. This is the magic of theory. As further examples of the generality of the theory, the relationship of the general theory to ongoing research with the evolution of flying insects is explored in the next chapter, then in Chapter 12 the theory is applied to two vessels of antiquity.

*References for Chapter 10 only:*


1. Bradfield, W.S. "On the Design of Radical High Speed Sailing Vessels." *Marine Technology*, Jan 1980. 17 (1).
2. Brown, Stuart F. "Breaking the Limits of Sailboat Speed." *Yachting*, April 1991.
3. Ellison, Michael. "25 Years of Sail." *SAIL*, January   1995.
4. IYRU (International Yacht Racing Union)/ World Speed Record Council 1995/1997. "1995/97 World Sailing Speed Record Rules Including Record Rules for Individually Attempted Passage Records." Royal Yachting Association, Hants, England.
5. Johnson, Peter. *Boating Facts and Feats*, New York: Sterling, 1976. p.22-23.
6. Long, Russel. "A Long Shot." *SAIL*, June 1992.
7. Pickthall, Barry. "Australian Fast Lady Out to Break 50 Knots" *The Times*, London, 12 Oct 1993.
8. "Australians go fast." *SAIL*, May 1993.

# Chapter 11 - The General Theory and the Evolution of Flying Insects ( Allocapnia Vivipara )

This chapter explores the relationship of the general theory to ongoing research on the possible evolutionary transition of sailing insects to flying insects. The general theory is applied to sailing stoneflies. James Marden and Melissa Kramer have studied the sailing stonefly (*Allocapnia vivipara*). Their experimental data suggests that "sailing has a greater potential to drive the evolution of insects wings than does aerial gliding" (1995, p 333). The results of applying the general theory to this field of study show the generality of the theory. The results of the application support the hypothesis that sailing stoneflies may have preceded flying stoneflies. The results show a small change in course by the sailing stonefly can lead to higher sailing speeds and possibly put the stonefly in a position for, as suggested here, a hop, flap, and glide sequence that may also have just preceded flapping powered flight.

The general theory assumes that fluid flow over and about a sailing object produces a righting moment required of the object and that the object is able to produce a righting moment available to counter the righting moment required during steady, straight line, translational motion on a flat surface. It also assumes that there are lift and drag force ratios connected to an apparent wind generated by the source pair of object velocity and true wind speed. All these assumptions play a part in the application to the sailing stonefly.

This chapter presents mostly a qualitative application of the theory. Quantitative predictions from assumptions are made to demonstrate qualitative aspects of the sailing theory. The results of the application represent one link in the chain to possible theories for evolution of nonflapping sailing stoneflies to flapping, flying stoneflies. Also, in relation to the sailing stonefly, the chapter shows one way in which results of the theory can be used to generate a resistance curve and the theory application shows how sailing speeds can be increased by sailing at true wind angles above direct downwind. It is from the standpoint of first, achieving the increased sailing speeds at a higher sailing angle, that the additional flap, hop, and glide sequence link to flying is proposed.

The stonefly has two forward wings and two aft wings on an elongated body supported by 4 feet, two each side. There are antennae in front and an aft appendage. They raise their wings in response to gusts of wind for sailing. The assumed wing orientation of a typical female stonefly is shown in Figure 11-1. Table 11-1 provides additional stonefly characteristics necessary for applying the theory. In Table 11-1, downwind $S.A./\Delta$ is based on the estimated downwind projected sail area of the raised aft wings. The $(B/H)_{maximum}$ estimated for the theory use is for a stonefly with horizontal wings that provide no lift, up or down; but the stonefly is sailing hull-afly on its two same-side feet, where those feet have become the same as one of the two hulls of a catamaran as the stonefly sails above direct downwind to a true wind course angle of 135°.

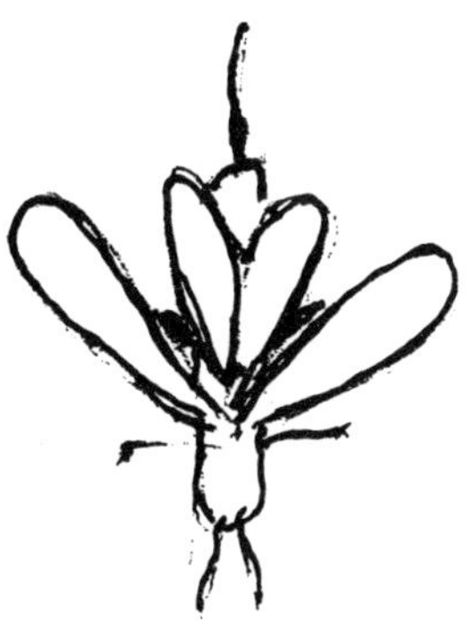


Figure 11-1
Female Stonefly, Wing Raised

| | |
|---|---|
| Displacement weight $(\Delta)$ : | $5.07 \times 10^{-6}$ lbs (2.3 mg) |
| *(B/H)* maximum | |
| (Horizontal wings, zero lift): | 1.0 |
| | |
| *S.A./$\Delta$,* Direct downwind : | 11.88 ft $^2$/lb |
| length of wings : | 0.5 cm (0.0164 ft) |
| length of body : | 0.5 cm (0.01643 ft) |

Table 11-1
Female Stonefly Characteristics

General views of the stonefly on a smooth flat surface, $\Sigma$, for two courses, a direct downwind sailing course and a true wind course of 135°, are shown in Figure 11-2, along with the associated source pairs of speed required of the theory. The source pair for $_{\theta}TW = 135°$ is with a boat speed that results in an apparent wind angle of 90°. The orientation of the horizontal forward wings are such that when the apparent wind angle is 90°, then the flow across the windward wing can result in the nonflapping wing developing aerodynamic lift and drag. At $\beta = 90°$ the drag will not slow the stonefly, and the lift, either up or down, could be used to balance it in roll (see Figure 11-3). While the development of lift is a possibility for increasing the $(B/H)_{maximum}$ that the stonefly can use in sailing for purposes of demonstrating the theory here, the lift is assumed to be zero, and balancing forces are from the weight of the stonefly alone, so that at "hull-afly" $(B/H)$ is approximately 1. See Figure 11-4.

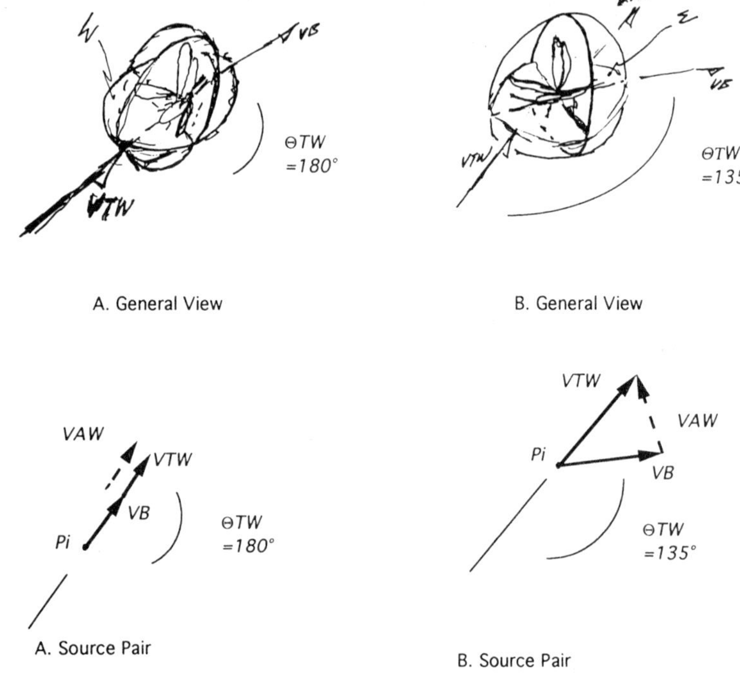


Figure 11-2
General View of Stoneflies Sailing at
A. $\Theta TW = 180°$ and
B. $\Theta TW = 135°$ with Corresponding Source Pairs

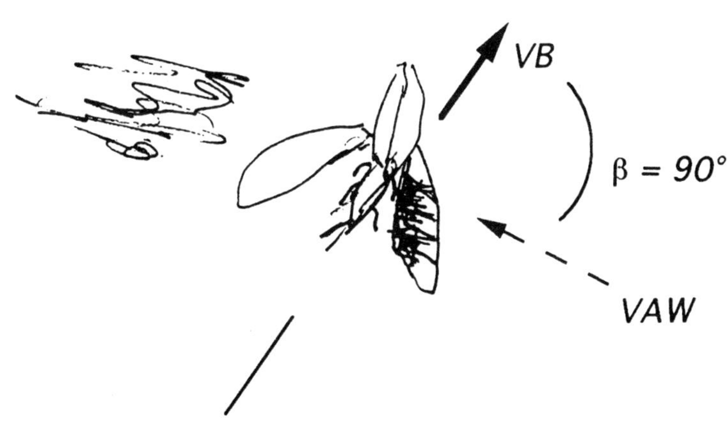


Figure 11-3
Apparent Wind Flow, For ß = 90°,
Over Horizontal Nonflapping Stonefly Wings

$F_H$

$H$

$\mu H$

$B_{STANCE}$

$\ell_1$

$W_{stonefly}$

$\ell_1 \approx \frac{1}{2} B_{stance}$

$\mu \approx 1$

$\Delta_T = W_{stonefly}$

with,
No Lift on Horizontal Wings

$$\text{Righting Moment} = \ell_1 \, W_{stonefly}$$
$$= \frac{1}{2} B_{stance} \, W_{stonefly}$$

$$Arm_{i_{max}} = \frac{\frac{1}{2} B_{stance} \, \Delta_T}{\Delta_T} = \frac{1}{2} B_{stance}$$

$$\frac{2 \, Arm_i}{H} \approx \frac{B_{stance}}{H}$$

$$B \approx H$$

$$\left(\frac{B}{H}\right)_{equivalent} = \frac{2 \, Arm_i}{H} \approx 1$$

Figure 11-4
*B/H*equivalent Calculation for Nonflapping Stoneflies

Even with these reasonable assumptions, there are still difficulties in using this sailing theory to make anything but very rough predictions for the stonefly. The difficulties are the following:

1. The exact positions of the forward semihorizontal wings and the aft vertical wings are not known.
2. The true wind velocity in the vicinity of the sailing stoneflies of the Marden and Kramer experiment is probably different from the true wind velocity they measured and reported above the stonefly's sailing surface. The true wind for the downwind sailing stoneflies was measured at 0.082 ft (2.5 cm), the stonefly's mast height is about 0.016 ft (0.5 cm). It is well known that there is a gradient to the wind from 100 feet above a smooth surface to the smooth surface. Figure 11-5 presents a profile of wind speed above a flat surface based on measurements above smooth snow and flat water (PNA VII 1988, p.33, Figure 31). The dashed lines in the figure are a continuation of the profile to zero speed at ground zero and a linear approximation of the continued profile section.

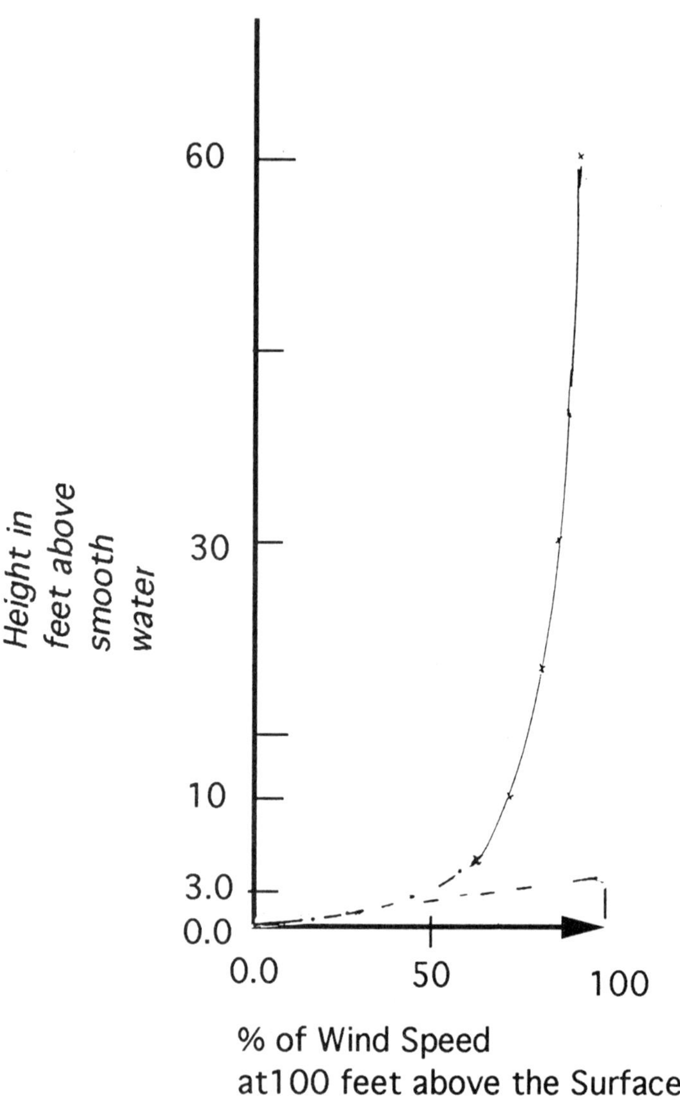


Figure 11-5
Profiles of True Wind Speed ( PNA, 1988 )

152

For purposes of demonstrating this application of the general theory, it is assumed that the true wind speed on the theoretical flat surface, $\Sigma$, is 1/2 of the measured reported true wind of the Marden-Kramer experiments. The assumptions of downwind sail area to displacement ratio of 11.88 ft2/lb, $(B/H)_{maximum}$ hull-afly = 1, true wind velocity of 1/2 the measured velocity of the experiments with a driving force coefficient of 1 downwind, and a drag to lift ratio of 0.5 for the vertical wings at speed and at true wind course of 135° are sufficient to produce driving force per pound displacement for the nonflapping stoneflies. The fraction of mast height heeling arm, $\mu$, from Figure 11-4 is taken as 1.

For downwind wind sailing, driving force per pound displacement at true wind speeds of 0.2 knots, 0.68 knots, and 1.27 knots is shown in Figures 11-6A and 11-6B. Figure 11-6B also shows a resistance curve for the stoneflies of the experiment produced by marking on the driving force curves the measured speeds of the experiment. (This method can also be used for modern sailboats.) This resistance curve is used in combination with the driving forces generated for a true wind course angle of 135° from the theory to produce predicted equilibrium speeds for the stoneflies able to achieve a true wind course of 135°. In the Marden-Kramer experiments, it would be necessary for the stoneflies to change course from downwind to $\odot TW = 135°$. In nature, a gusty wind could produce the same result as a sudden change in course, just as it does sometimes for sailboats.

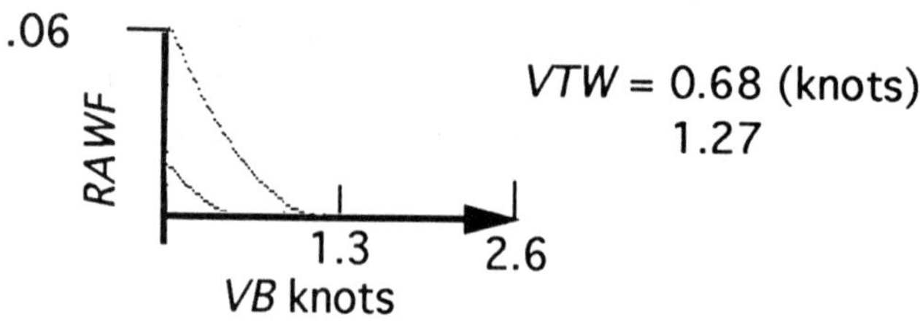


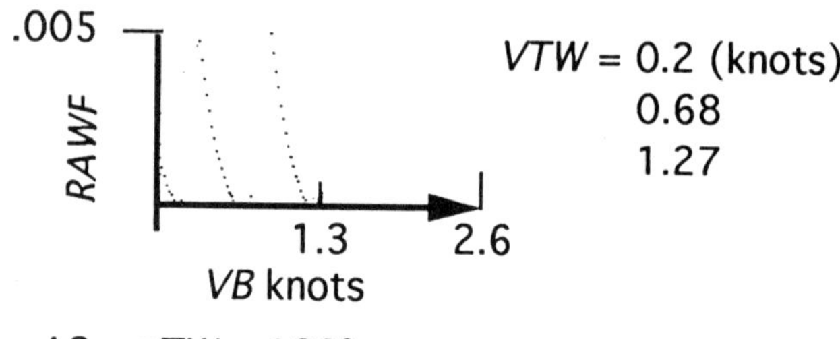


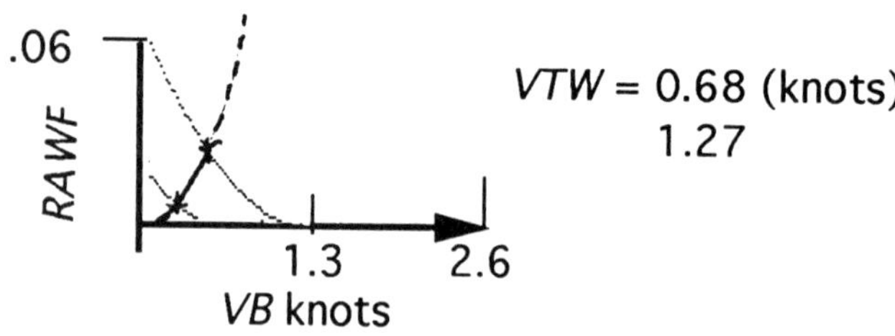


Figure 11-6
A. Stonefly Driving Force Downwind,
$C_F$ = 1.0, $S.A./\Delta$ = 11 ft2/lb.
B. Resistance Curve Constructed, --- Line Is Assumed Extension

The driving forces per pound displacement for a true wind course angle of 135° are shown in Figures 11-7A and 11-7B. The previously estimated resistance curve is added to Figure 11-7B to produce estimated sailing speeds for the stonefly at a true wind angle of 135°.

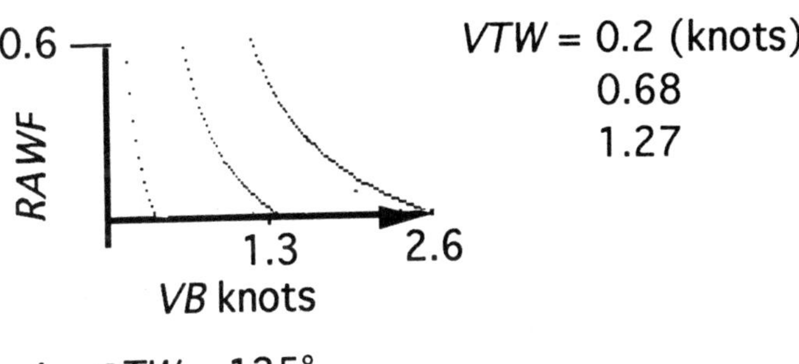


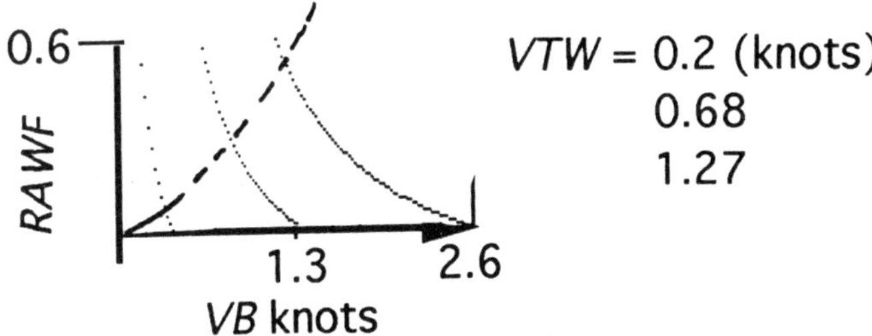


Figure 11-7
A. Stonefly *RAWF* at ΘTW = 135° ($C_D/C_L$ = 0.5, B/H = 1.0)
B. Resistance Curve Added to *RAWF* to
Estimated Sailing Speeds Possible

Table 11-2 presents a summary of reported measured wind speeds, assumed true wind speeds for the theory application, measured stonefly downwind speeds reported, and estimated speeds possible from the theory for $\Theta TW = 135°$. The measured downwind speeds and the estimated $\Theta TW = 135°$ speeds are also plotted versus assumed true wind speeds in Figure 11-8. It is interesting to note from the inspection of Figure 11-8 that some ability to sail other than downwind could result in higher sailing speeds for the nonflapping stonefly. These higher sailing speeds at the higher course (more windward) could activate lift and drag capabilities for the nonflapping vertical and horizontal wings. (See Figure 11-3.) Furthermore, should the antenna of the stonefly act as a wind flow and orientation sensor with feedback to the horizontal wings such that they rotate to provide lift and roll stabilization in a self-leveling system with the horizontal wings acting like the foils on sailboats, like *Longshot* (see Chapter 10), then the stonefly can increase its sailing *B/H* above that for body weight balance alone and attain higher "take-off" speeds just before flapping.

| Reported Measured Wind at 2.5 cm height | Assumed True Wind at Stonefly Mast Height, 0.5 cm | Measured Downwind Speed | Estimated Speed for $\Theta TW=135°$ $B/H = 1.0$ $C_D/C_L = 0.5$ $\mu = 1.0$ |
|---|---|---|---|
| 2.53 knots (1.3 ms$^{-1}$) | 1.27 knots (0.65 ms$^{-1}$) | 0.48 knots (24.7 cms$^{-1}$) | 1.4 knots (0.72 ms$^{-1}$) |
| 1.36 knots (0.7 ms$^{-1}$) | 0.68 knots (0.35 ms$^{-1}$) | 0.29 knots (15 cms$^{-1}$) | 1.0 knots (0.51 ms$^{-1}$) |
| 0.39 knots (0.2 ms$^{-1}$) | 0.2 knots (0.1 ms$^{-1}$) | 0.17 knots (9 cms$^{-1}$) | 0.4 knots (0.21 ms$^{-1}$) |

Table 11-2
Summary of Stonefly Speeds

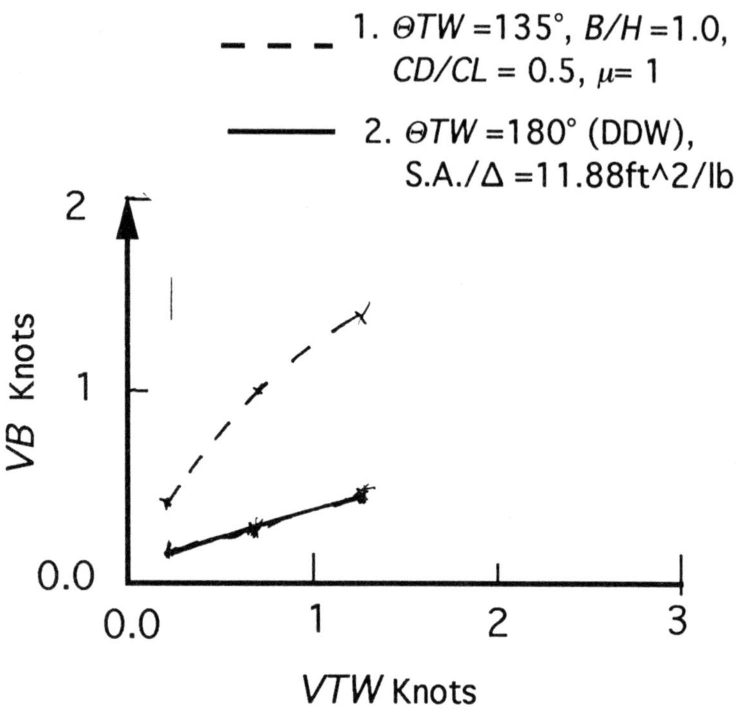



Figure 11-8
1. $VB_{estimate}$ vs. *VTW* for Sailing Course ($\Theta TW$ = 180°)
2. Measured *VB* (Marden and Kramer) vs. *VTW* for Direct Downward Sailing ($\Theta TW$ = 180°)

To proceed from the point of nonflapping wing sailing speed to full flapping wing flight is another matter. Should the nonflapping stonefly achieve a balanced hull-afly sailing speed and also learn to achieve even higher sailing speeds with horizontal wing axis rotation control to control the angle of attack, then perhaps the next step to flying could be a flap of the horizontal wings, giving it an airborne hop followed by an initial evolutionary glide back to the surface of the earth. Once it hops, it jumps into a higher true wind layer of air flow which may or may not aid its transition to flapping flying. Once airborne, how it glides or flaps back to the surface is subject matter for other investigators who, at this time, continue to research just how flapping wing insects fly. For example, see Ellington et al. 1996, "Leading Edge Vortices in Insect Flight."

This general theory application has been to female stoneflies. "Females are uniformly long-winged (70-105% of body length), whereas males are mostly short-winged (33-65% of body length)." (Marden, p.322). It is worth noting that if the male has the same stance width, $B_{stance}$, as the female, it could sail at a larger $(B/H)_{equivalent}$ ratio, making it possible for it to sail in higher winds than the female. The significance of this is left to the biologists.

With the production of estimated sailing speeds for stoneflies, a micronistic application of the theory for sailboat objects has been advanced. In Chapters 8-10, macronistic applications for modern sailboats were presented. In the next chapter the theory continues to show its generality. Two more macronistic applications of the theory are presented. The performance capabilities of two sailboats of antiquity are estimated and the possibility of an ancient universal sailmaker conversant with the theory is advanced and proven.

*References for Chapter 11 only:*

1. Marden, James H., and Kramer, Melissa G. "Locomotor Performance of Insects with Rudimentary Wings," *Nature*, Vol. 377, Sept. 28, 1995. pp. 332-334.

2. Ellington, Charles P., Vandenburg, Coen, Willmoth, Alexander P., and Thomas, Adrian R. "Leading Edge Vortices in Insect Flight," *Nature*, Vol. 384, December 26, 1996. pp. 626-630.

160

# Chapter 12 - The General Theory, Vessels of Antiquity, Sailmakers and Summary

This chapter will show again that all that is necessary to apply the primitive of the theory to a specific sailboat object is to identify the trio, $\mu$, $B/H$, and, $C_D/C_L$ for the sailing object. The sailing characteristics of two vessels of antiquity are explored in terms of their speed determining factors from the standpoint of the general theory. The first ancient vessel explored in terms of the theory is a Greek pentekenter-sailor from ca. 500 BC, which could be called an auxiliary oar-powered sailing ship. The next is a "root boat," a Chinese sailing raft, one of the very first types of sailboat, with what is, apparently, a water-tight aft bowl cockpit built in the raft. There is sufficient archeological information about these vessels to apply the general theory to them. A discussion of the first vessel's sailing abilities proceeds to a hypothetical line of thought on how an ancient sailmaker might have thought about the performance of the vessel were he conversant with the theory. Proof of the possibility of such an ancient sailmaker is provided with a special illustration of a page from the theory.

Boats of antiquity were sailing vessels for commerce, exploration, simple point-to-point transportation, and fighting battles at sea. What were their exact constructions, configurations, shapes, sail-rigs, and crewing (manning)? These are significant questions. Passages from translations of Aristotle, Virgil, and others, as represented in *Ships and Seamanship in the Ancient World* by Lionel Casson (1971, pp 275-276), provide a basis for a description of how some ancient vessels were sailed. Such questions, however, cannot be fully answered. The general theory cannot answer them either, but it can provide insight into the driving forces of the wind for these vessels.

The process of predicting driving forces for all vessels requires important ratios to be identified. Possible equivalent catamaran beam-to-mast height ratios ($B/H$), the fraction of mast height heeling arm ($\mu$), and drag to lift ratios ($C_D/C_L$) for the sail-rig. For the two examples presented, these are identified or estimated. *B/H* maximum is an especially important ratio since it relates to ancient sailboats ability to stay upright, stay afloat, and reach their destinations.

The development of the sailboat can be described as an evolutionary path that is marked and understood in terms of the general
theory. Near the beginning of the path is a square-rigged,
single-pole-mast sailing vessel. The first vessel of antiquity that the
general theory is applied to is a vessel very much like an Egyptian
vessel of ca. 2500 BC (see Casson, 1971, Figure 18). It is a
hemiolia of 500 BC described by R. B. Nelson in *War Fleets of
Antiquity* (1973, pp. 18-19). This sailing ship is "very similar to
the two banked pentekenter" (p. 19). "It had a crew of 52 rowers,
each with one oar, 14 of whom form the mast striking party with
others of 10 approx." Nelson's hemiolia had an overall length of
70 feet and a waterline length of about 57 feet. The hemiolia is
illustrated in Figure 12-1, along with some calculated estimates of
factors for use with the general theory.  It combined the pulling
power of oarsmen with the driving forces of a square rigged
single-pole-mast, shallow draft sailing vessel.

The displacement for this first vessel is not provided by Nelson,
but by assuming a full shape with a block coefficient of 0.8,
estimates for volume displacement, $V$, and weight displacement ,
$\Delta$, are made. The block coefficient is the ratio of volume displacement to waterline length, times the waterline beam, times the
draft. Thus, the volume displaced is the block coefficient, times
the length waterline, times the beam waterline, times the draft.
Then the displacement weight is the density of water times the
volume displacement. The results are shown in Figure 12-1, along
with corresponding length-to-volume-to-the-one-third-power ratio,
$L/V^{1/3}$, and sail area, $S.A.$ (ft$_2$) to weight displacement in pounds
ratio, $S.A./\Delta$, all estimated for the hemiolia  and useful in making
performance predictions.

$\mu$

Sail Top Position  ~ 0.9
Sail Lowest        ~ 0.68
Sail as Shown      ~ 0.83

Sail
 Geometric Aspect Ratio = 0.3
Hull
 Geometric Aspect Ratio = 0.05

$$(B/H)\text{maximum} = \frac{2\,ARM\text{maximum}}{H} =$$

Sail Top Position $= \dfrac{2 \times 1}{35} = 0.06$

Sail Lowest Position $= \dfrac{2 \times 1}{15} = 0.13$

Sail Position as Shown $= \dfrac{2 \times 1}{30} = 0.07$

*S.A./Akeelhull = 6.2*

*Block Coefficient $= \dfrac{Vhemiolia}{LwL \times Bwl \times Draft}$*

*if Block Coefficient = 0.8 (a full shape bow to stern)*
*then, Vhemiolia = 0.8 x (57ft x 10 ft x 2.5 ft)*
*= 1140 ft^3*

and Δhemiolia = 1140 ft^3 x 64 lbs/ft^3 = 72,960 lbs
and ∀^1/3 = 10.42 ft
L/∀^1/3  = 5.47
S.A./Δ  $= \dfrac{40\ ft \times 10\ ft}{72{,}960\ lbs} = 0.0055$ ft^2/lbs

Figure 12-1
A. Calculations for General Theory Factors
B. Factors Based on Block Coefficient = 0.8

Besides the information in Figures 12-1, it is also necessary to estimate the drag to lift ratio, $C_D/C_L$, for the hemiolia rig on course. Wind tunnel results for a single square-rigged Proelss-rig are reported by W. Warner and H. M. Kossa in "Updating an Ancient Art—Research and Development Toward Modern Wind Powered Cargo Ships" (STAR SYMPOSIUM, SNAME, 25 May 1977). Figure 12-2 shows the single-mast Proelss-rig measured $C_D$ and $C_L$ values for a rig of geometric aspect ratio of approximately 2 and effective aspect ratio of about 4. Figure 12-3 shows an estimated $C_D/C_L$ versus angle of attack for this rig. [The estimates are based on a comparison of Figure 12-2 and wind tunnel information from Marchaj (1979, p. 587, Figure 3.32) to identify estimated angles of attack for the $C_D/C_L$ of Figure 12-2.]

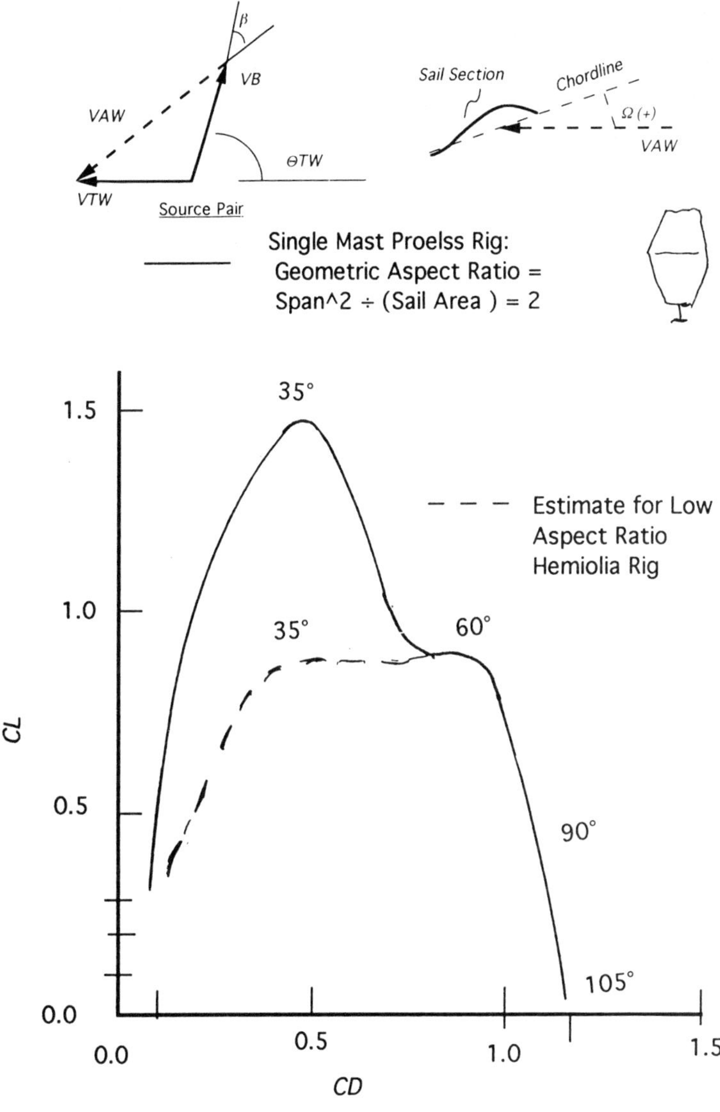


Figure 12-2
Drag and Lift Coefficients for a Single Mast Square Rig,
a Proelss Rig (Warner and Kossa, 1977).
Effective Aspect Ratio = 4

165

While the Proelss-rig data is for an effective aspect ratio of about 4, the hemiolia rig has a geometric aspect ratio of 0.3 for an effective aspect ratio of 0.6. Lanchester-Prandtl wing theory, as reported in Ira H. Abbott and Albert E. Von Doenhoff, *Theory of Wing Sections, Including a Summary of Airfoil Data,* provides a method to estimate drag coefficients, $C_D$, and angles of attack, $\Omega$ (in radians), for a wing of one effective aspect ratio, $AR_{eff2}$, from data for a wing of another effective aspect ratio, $AR_{eff1}$.

$$C_{D2} = C_{D1} + (C_{L1}^2/\pi)\,(1/AR_{eff2} - 1/AR_{eff1})$$

$$\Omega_2 = \Omega_1 + (C_{L1}/\pi)\,(1/AR_{eff2} - 1/AR_{eff1})$$

From an inspection of these relations, it is clear that a low aspect ratio rig will result in a higher drag coefficient for the same coefficient of lift as that for a higher aspect ratio rig, and that this drag coefficient will occur at a larger angle of attack. Thus a low aspect ratio rig results in a higher drag-to-lift ratio at a higher angle of attack, $\Omega$, for the same coefficient of lift as the coefficient of lift for a higher aspect ratio rig (up to about 35 degrees angle of attack). The hemiolia is a low-aspect-ratio rig. Its estimated drag-to-lift capabilities are represented by dashed lines in Figures 12-2 and 12-3. When using the information in Figure 12-3, it is important to be cognizant of the angle relationship shown in Chapter 2, $\Omega = \beta - \lambda - \delta.$

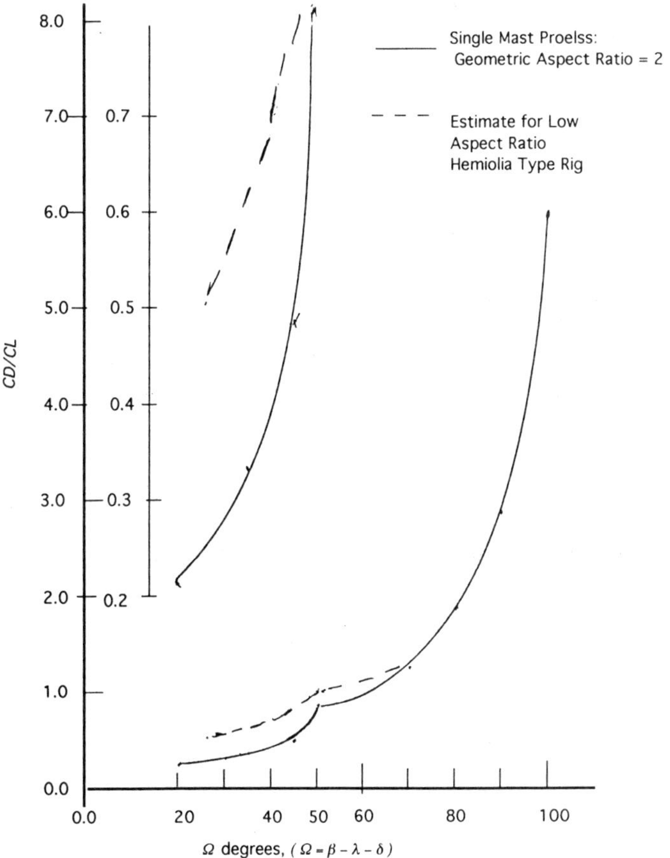


Figure 12-3
Estimates for $C_D/C_L$ versus Angle of Attack
for Proelss Rig (Solid Line) and Hemiolia Rig (Dashed Line)

To represent the hemiolia's driving force per pound displacement capabilities from the wind, a true wind speed, $VTW$, of 15 knots for two true wind courses, $\ominus TW$, are chosen. Because the hemiolia doesn't have much of a keel, it must depend on the blunt hull to develop balancing side forces for courses of about 90°, and does so at large leeway angles, $\lambda$ (greater than 10°), reducing driving force capabilities and at the same time increasing resistance forces of the craft on courses upwind ($\ominus TW < 90°$), drastically reducing speed capabilities on those courses. As a consequence, it couldn't sail up wind. Thus the two true wind courses that represent the hemiolia's driving force capabilities are for direct downwind and crosswind. For crosswind $RAWF$, a $B/H$ of one-third the maximum for sails up was selected (the crew probably wasn't anxious to sail on the edge required of maximum beam-to-mast-height-ratio use), and a drag-to-lift ratio for the sail-rig of 0.5 was selected. For downwind $RAWF$, a sail area to displacement ratio, ($S.A./\Delta$), of 0.0055 was used with a driving force coefficient, $C_F$, of 1.0.

Figure 12-4 displays the driving force per pound displacement results for the hemiolia crosswind and downwind in 15 knots of true wind. In Figures 12-5 and 12-6, speed capabilities for these courses are found by adding estimated resistance curves to the driving force curves. The added high resistance curve (based on the submerged frontal area of the hull) in Figure 12-5 produces equilibrium sailboat speeds of 2.2 knots downwind and 4.3 knots crosswind. In Figure 12-6 an added low resistance curve (based on Figure 7-1 in Chapter 7, with $L/V^{1/3} = 5$) produces equilibrium boat speeds of 3 plus knots downwind and 6 knots crosswind. Thus it is found in 15 knots of true wind speed, that the hemiolia's downwind speed is between 2.2 knots and 3 knots, and its crosswind speed is between 4.3 and 6 knots.

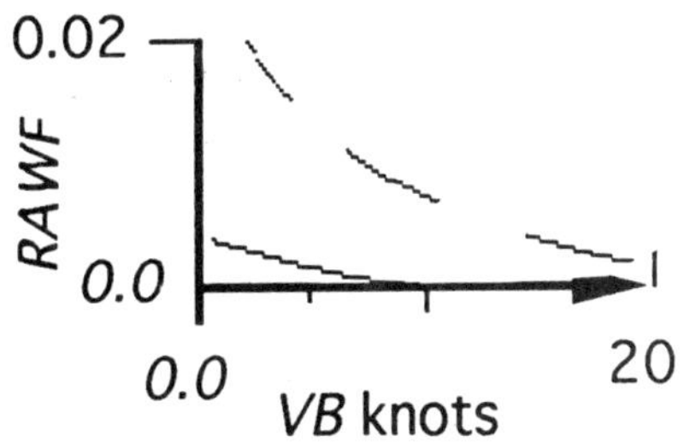


Figure 12-4
Driving Force (*RAWF*) for Hemiolia Downwind,
$\Theta TW$ = 180° (Solid Line)
and Crosswind, $\Theta TW$ = 180° (Dashed Line)

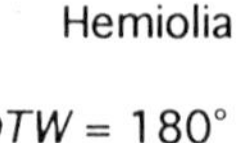


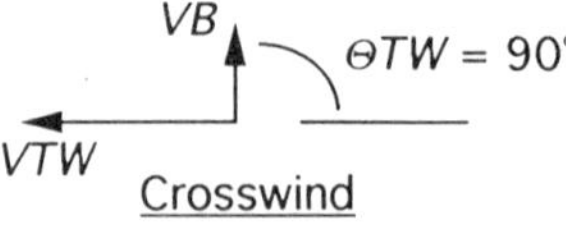


$VTW = 15$ knots

Equilibrium Boat Speeds

— — — $\Theta TW = \phantom{0}90°$, VBequilibrium $= 4.3$ knots
———— $\Theta TW = 180°$, VBequilibrium $= 2.2$ knots

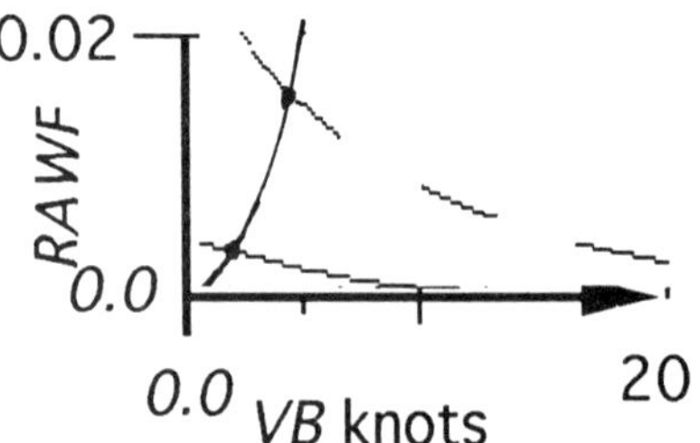


Figure 12-5
High Resistance Curve Added to Driving Force Curves
of Figure 12-4
$A_{frontalhull}/\Delta = 0.00026$ ft2/lb

Hemiolia

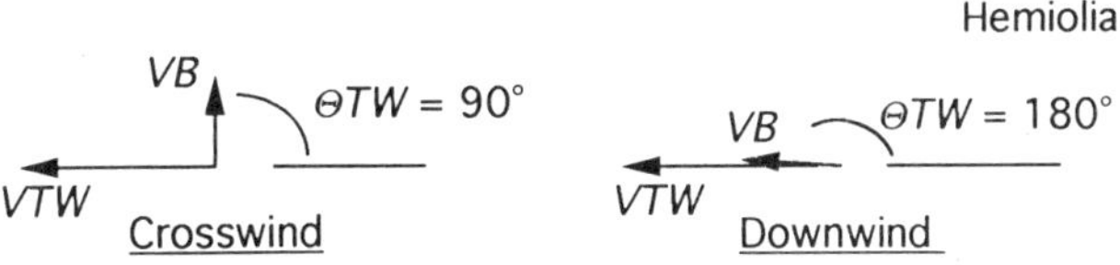


*VTW* = 15 knots

Equilibrium Boat Speeds

– –  Θ*TW* =  90°, *VBequilibrium* ~= 6 knots
——  Θ*TW* = 180°, *VBequilibrium*  = 3+ knots

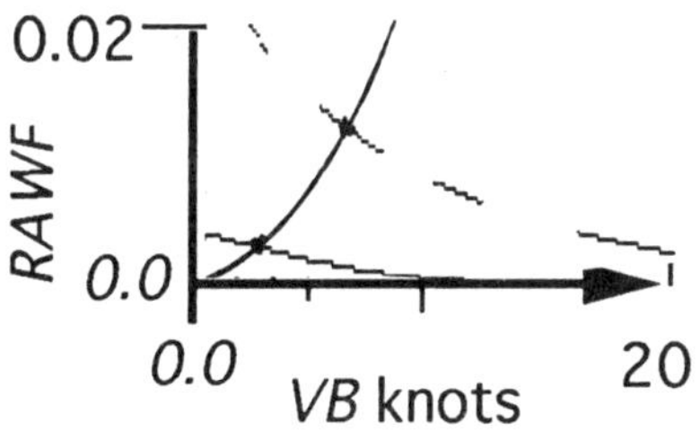


Figure 12-6
Low Resistance Curve Added to Driving Force Curves
of Figure 12-4

Suppose there was an ancient sailmaker who knew both the hemiolia and the general theory. How would he or she think about the hemiola? He or she see would see that the panel sail could be set at the top or lowered to the deck. In heavy winds he or she would think that lowering it to the deck would change $C_D/C_L$ and reduce $\mu$. It might reduce $B/H$, but the wind would rise and increase $B/H$. In light winds, the sailmaker might think about raising the yard arm to the top and increasing $B/H$, but $\mu$ might also increase and $C_D/C_L$ would increase as well.

He or she would always wonder why the vessel would sail crosswind and downwind but not upwind at all. The vessel would wear about to change course from one side of the wind to the other. [Wear about means changing tack (course) from one side of the wind to the other by going downwind first.] The sailmaker would wonder how to get his owner's merchantman vessel a little more safety from an adverse wind and a leeshore. Or on a war ship, he would wonder how to get more ability to get the boat above crosswind in battle and give the battling warriors a tactical advantage to windward at a position from which to bear down and ram the enemy ship downwind that is still feathering its oars or pulling frantically into the wind.

In medium wind conditions, he or she would think about possibly cutting the sails a little deeper, a little baggier, to keep them low and maybe increase $B/H$ without increasing $\mu$ and $C_D/C_L$ and get a little more speed crosswind. Such is how the ancient sailmaker might think if he or she had known the general theory then.

R.B. Nelson says of this sailing ship, "When attacking a merchant ship, the hemiolia would approach under oars and sail, possibly as fast as 10 knots, or twice the speed of the best merchantman" (1973, p.19). From the resulting sailing speed predictions, it is clear that oarsmen added from 6 to 7 knots of speed to the sailing speed of this ship. Should a warship similarly outfitted be seeking escape, after rowing as hard as they could, the scantily clad lee-side rowers would jump to the windward-high rail and add 10% to 12% to the ship's $B/H$ during an attack, and perhaps 1/2 to 3/4 of a knot of speed (see Chapter 8) to a safe haven and so save themselves from the enemy.

The second vessel of antiquity to which the general theory is applied is the Chinese raft. The Chinese raft is a strikingly different vessel from the hemiolia. It was built of various materials, including wooden poles from which it obtained buoyancy. In *Archaeology of the Boat* (1976, p. 97), Basil Greenhill describes the raft boat as "the first root" of earliest boats. Greenhill thinks that "the rafts have played a part in the evolution of some Chinese boats and ships" (p.99). The Chinese raft boat selected to demonstrate the general theory is based on a photo of a model in the National Maritime Museum (p.101, Figure 53). It has a square-rigged sail with a drop keel (daggerboard), steering oars, and a round tub cockpit, possibly watertight. The daggerboard keel, like a leeboard on early Dutch and Viking vessels, gives the sailing raft the ability to sail with reduced leeway angles on all courses, but especially on courses above crosswind.

The Chinese raft of wooden pole construction, with factors calculated for the general theory's use, is shown in Figure 12-7. Raw wind forces (driving force per pound displacement from the theory) for this early raft sailing craft are presented in Figure 12-8 for crosswind ($\theta TW = 90°$) courses and $VTW = 15$ knots. For the crosswind driving forces, a $B/H$ of 0.035 (1/2 the maximum), a $\mu$ of 0.75 and a $C_D /C_L$ of 0.5 were used for the theory. In Figure 12-9, a high resistance curve [frontal hull area (ft$^2$) to pound hull displacement = 0.00071] and a low resistance curve ($L/\forall^{1/3} = 5$) (see Chapter 7) have been added to the driving force curves of Figure 12-8. The monotonically increasing resistance curves intersect the raw wind force curves of the theory at equilibrium boat speeds. The equilibrium speeds found for the low resistance curve are a lumbering 3.1 knots downwind and a faster, trotting 6.1 knots crosswind.

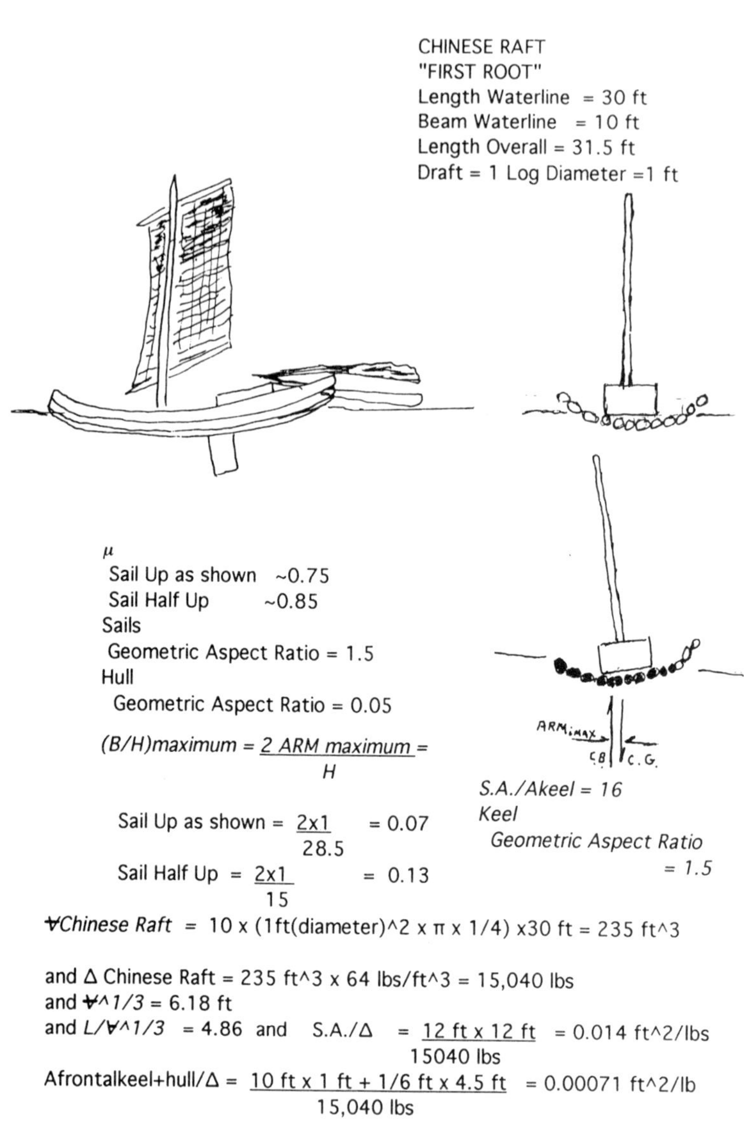


$\forall Chinese\ Raft = 10 \times (1ft(diameter)^2 \times \pi \times 1/4) \times 30\ ft = 235\ ft^3$

and $\Delta$ Chinese Raft = 235 ft^3 x 64 lbs/ft^3 = 15,040 lbs
and $\forall^{1/3}$ = 6.18 ft
and $L/\forall^{1/3}$ = 4.86  and   S.A./$\Delta$  $= \dfrac{12\ ft \times 12\ ft}{15040\ lbs} = 0.014\ ft^2/lbs$

Afrontalkeel+hull/$\Delta$ = $\dfrac{10\ ft \times 1\ ft + 1/6\ ft \times 4.5\ ft}{15,040\ lbs}$ = 0.00071 ft^2/lb

Figure 12-7
Calculations for Chinese Raft for Use with the Theory

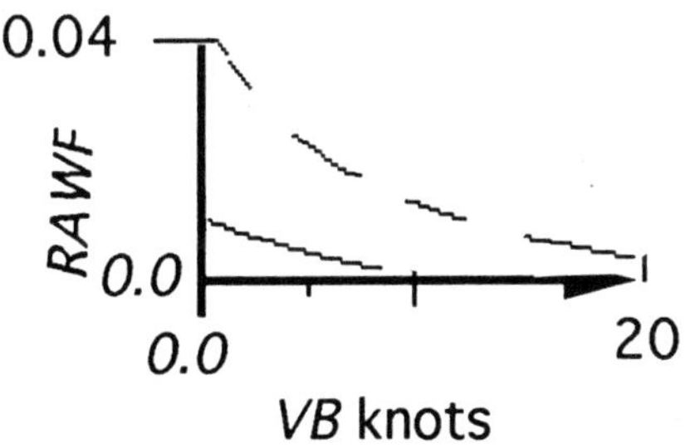

Figure 12-8
Chinese Raft Driving Forces (*RAWF*) for Downwind,
Θ*TW* = 180° (Solid Line)
and Crosswind, Θ*TW* = 90° (Dashed Line)

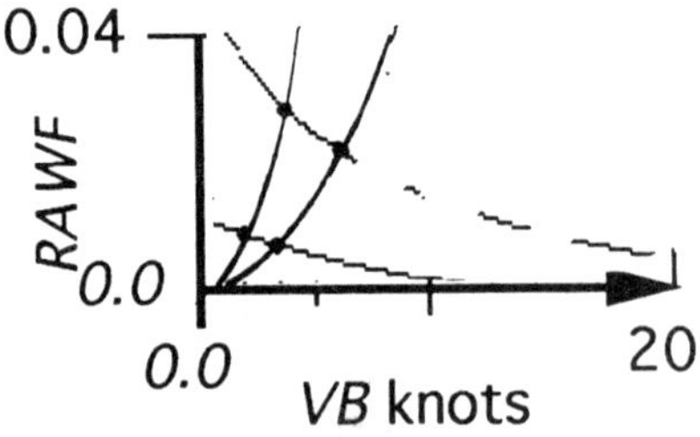

$VB$     $\Theta TW = 90°$
$VTW$    Crosswind

$VB$    $\Theta TW = 180°$
$VTW$    Downwind

$VTW = 15$(knots)

— — —    $\Theta TW = 90°$

     *VBequilibrium*

       High resistance = 3.5 knots
       Low resistance = 6.1 knots

————    $\Theta TW = 180°$

     *VBequilibrium*

       High resistance = 2 knots
       Low resistance = 3.1 knots

Figure 12-9
High Resistance Curve and Low Resistance Curve
Added to Driving Force Curves of Figure 12-8

The daggerboard made it possible for the Chinese craft to sail above a crosswind-truewind angle of 90°, possibly as high as $\Theta TW$ = 50-60°. Figure 12-10 presents driving forces for $\Theta TW$ = 60° with high resistance and low resistance curves added. (The factors for driving force from the theory are $B/H$ = 0.07 ($B/H_{max}$ for upwind sailing), $C_D/C_L$ = 0 0.5 and $\mu$ = 0.75.) On this windward point of sail, the equilibrium speed for a high resistance curve is 3.2 knots and for low resistance it is 5.3 knots, providing a range of possible speeds for this ancient craft sailing to weather.

Chinese Raft

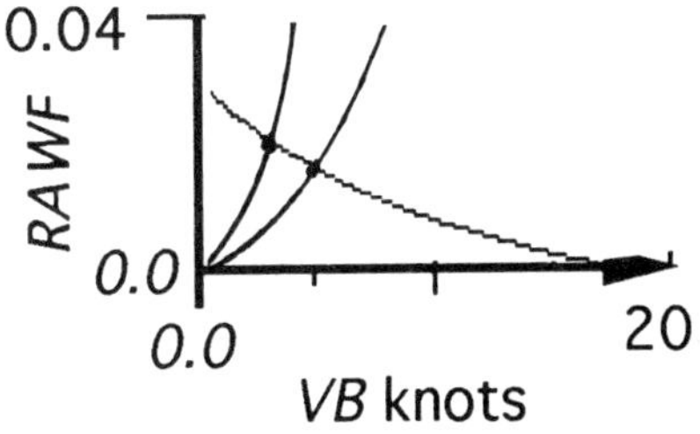


*VTW* = 15 (knots)

$\Theta TW$ = 60°

*VBequilibrium*

High resistance = 3.2 knots
Low resistance = 5.3 knots



Figure 12-10
High and Low Resistance Curves for the Chinese Raft
with Drop Keel Daggerboard Down Added to
Driving Forces for $\Theta TW$ = 60°

What would the ancient sailmaker think about this craft's abilities?  He would recognize the significant role of the daggerboard.
With the daggerboard up it sails like a hemiolia slipping
crosswind and sliding downwind.  With the daggerboard down
he would experience the boat's ability to take a windward bite
out of the wind and the sea and feel its tendency to heel to a
maximum $B/H$ soon. He might think about cutting the sails a little
flatter to delay reefing to half sail. He might wonder how the craft
would sail if it's hull were made water-tight by caulking the seams
between logs and then hollowing out the logs. For sure he would
think, if the caulking worked, then the craft could carry more
cargo on the same courses with more speed.

These boats of antiquity have been used to illustrate more applications of the general theory. Consideration has been given to how
the ancient sailmaker conversant with the general theory would
think. In contrast, another question can be posed: How would the
modern sailmaker, conversant with the general theory, think
about cutting new sails for a fast racing yacht or for a cruising
yacht? For a racing yacht, he might ask, What kind of winds
would the boat race in? How could it get the best $C_D/C_L$ for the
winds and courses it sails in? Could the lift distribution be lowered so $\mu$ is less while the driving force is kept the same, and the
same $B/H$ is attained in the same wind for the same true wind
course? For the cruising yacht he might ask, What would be the
range of wind speed for its sail? How important would a certain
course be? Increasing the draft may increase $B/H$ in lower winds
and more so in higher winds. It may also change $\mu$. Would the rig
not be so clean that the aspect ratio cut of the sails would not
effect the drag-to-lift ratio much? These are a few of the questions
a modern sailmaker might ask in terms of the general theory.

How would the modern designer think about the sailmaker's
proposal to the owner for a better sail? He would ask, "Does the
increased $B/H$ mean more heeled resistance in the same wind?
Does more heeled posture mean more leeway for critical courses?" More leeway might not result in a faster, more efficient vessel
or even more driving force for the speed. That is, the LH side of
Equation (13) might increase, but so would the RH side. (See
Chapter 5).  How would the balance point of speed change. And
then there are the dynamics. The general theory is built for action.

It is dynamic, but so is the sailboat. How are the dynamics (for the sailboat) changed with a change in sails? Is the boat already on the edge, like a high-performance fighter jet, constantly needing new trim by the crew, or are its dynamics solid as a freight train, always on track no matter what sails are set? So might the modern designer, conversant with the general theory, think.

How would the imagined ancient sailmaker have become conversant with the general theory? He would have spent time with a theorist-mentor and tuned in on some of Archimedes ideas (225 BC), turning them on their side, or, may have anticipated the ideas of Newton (1687) and Maxwell (1873). Suppose he had been aware of Archimedes of Alexandria's ideas, turned them on their side for sail forces with lifts and drags in the manner of Von Karman, ca. 1900, and Prandtl-Lanchester, ca. 1900 (Hoerner 1965), and knew some Pythagorean (540 BC) and Euclidean (300 BC) concepts to boot. Surely he would have had an edge on the competition. With a straight edge and compass in hand, and an army of apprentices, draftsmen, and journeymen to explore all the possibilities at hand, he would have done the exploration for the satisfaction of being able to do just that. A page from the general theory could have looked like the special-remarkable illustration in Figure 12-11.

Figure 12-11 illustrates the LH side of Raw Wind Forces and the RH side of resistance force per pound displacement in the direction of motion as could have been done on page or scratched in the sand by the ancient sailmaker. Of course, force resistance might be measured semi-quantitatively in human pull to move a hull along a canal with hemp lines and muscles of steel or in weight of gold coin. He also would have been conversant with the bird's-eye view illustrations of Figure 2-6 in Chapter 2 and of Figure 9-7 in Chapter 9, perhaps by drawing figures in smooth sand with a sharp stick. The drawing of the characters illustrated in Figure 12-11 with straight edge and bow compass is proof of what a page in the ancient sailmaker's notebook could have looked like. Figure 12-11 is a puzzle to be solved.

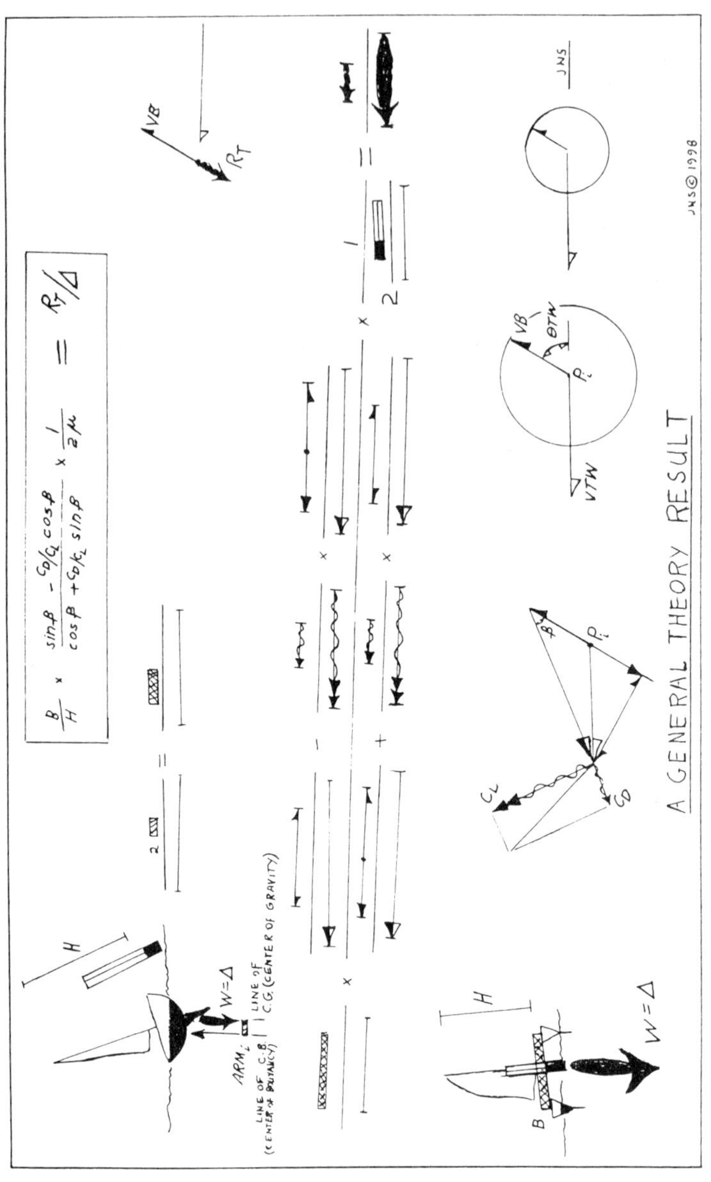


$$\frac{B}{H} \times \frac{\sin\beta - C_D/C_L \cos\beta}{\cos\beta + C_D/C_L \sin\beta} \times \frac{1}{2\mu} = R_T/\Delta$$

Figure 12-11
A General Theory Illustration with Straight Edge and Compass
LH Side Raw Wind Forces Balance RH Side Resistance Forces

The challenge goes on. One of the beautiful facets of the theory is that its results can be used with any aerodynamic and hydrodynamic theories that produce a drag-to-lift ratio for the sail-rig, $C_D/C_L$, a $B/H$ ratio for the postured hull and rig, an angle of attack, $\Omega$, for the sail-rig, a fraction, $\mu$, of the mast height, $H$, for the heeling arm of the keel-hull-rig combination, and a leeway angle, $\lambda$, for the hull-appendages, in a force balance (all six degrees of freedom or just three degrees of freedom as is current practice) at sailing speed, $VB$, on steady true wind course angle, $\Theta TW$, on smooth waters. While the challenge goes on, a stride forward in understanding how nature works its wonder with the sailboat has been made. Some of the black box mystery that surrounds the sailboat of nature has been removed by the formation and presentation of the general theory in Chapter 3, by the example applications of the general theory results in Chapters 8-12, and by the defining of the limits for sailboat speed in Chapter 9. The primitive mathematical expression wrought in Chapter 3 applies equally to vessels of antiquity, non-flapping stoneflies, low speed, medium speed and high speed sailboats, sailboards and hydrofoil craft, monohull and multihull, in short, it applies equally to any sailboat around the pond or around the world.

# Germane Bibliography
## (Reverse Chronological Order)


PNA. "Resistance, Propulsion, and Vibration," *Principles of Naval Architecture Vol.II*, SNAME, 1988.

Kerwin, J. E. "A Velocity Prediction Program for Ocean Racing Yachts Revised to June 1978," July 1986, Report #78-11 (1986 Coefficients). *H. Irving Pratt Ocean R&E Handicapping Project*, MIT.

Savitsky, D., and Gore, J.L. "Re-evaluation of the Planing Hull Form," *Journal of Hydronautics* ; vol. 14, no. 2, April 1980.

Hazen, George S. "A Model of Sail Aerodynamics for Diverse Rig Types," *The New England Sailing Yacht Symposium*, collected papers, March 22, 1980.

Norwood, Joseph Jr. *High Speed Sailing*, New York: Dodd, Mead, 1979.

Marchaj, C.A. *Aero-Hydrodynamics of Sailing*, New York: Dodd, Mead, 1979.

Scherer, Otto J. "Aerodynamics of High Performance Wing Sails," *Chesapeake Sailing Yacht Symposium*, SNAME section, 19 January 1974.

Milgram, J. H. *Sail Force Coefficients for Systematic Rig Variations*, SNAME T&R report R-10, 1971.

Hoerner, S. F. *Fluid Dynamic Drag*. Self-published, Lib of Cong. #64-19666, 1965.

Marchaj, C.A. *Sailing Theory and Practice*, New York: Dodd, Mead, 1965.

# Appendix I - Analytic Solutions
## for the Euclidian Triangle for $\beta$
## in Terms of $\ominus TW$, $VB$, and $VTW$

The velocity triangle composed at the apparent wind angle, $\beta$, in terms of the true wind angle, $\ominus TW$, and line lengths of boat speed, $VB$ and true wind speed, $VTW$, is an Euclidian Triangle. Analytic solutions for the Euclidian Triangle have been known since at least 300 BC.

According to Boyer's *History of Mathematics* (p. 124), The propositions 12 and 13 below, from Book II of Euclid's *Elements*, circa 300 BC, "became know as the law of cosines for plane triangles:

Proposition 12

In obtuse-angled triangles, the square of the side subtending the obtuse angle is greater than the squares on the sides containing the obtuse angle by twice the rectangle contained by one of the sides about the obtuse angle, namely that on which the perpendicular falls, and the straight line cut off outside by the perpendicular toward the obtuse angle.

Proposition 13

In acute-angled triangles, the square on the side subtending the acute angle is less than the squares on the sides containing the acute angle by twice the rectangle contained by one of the sides about the acute angle, namely that on which the perpendicular falls, and straight line cut off within by the perpendicular toward the acute angle."

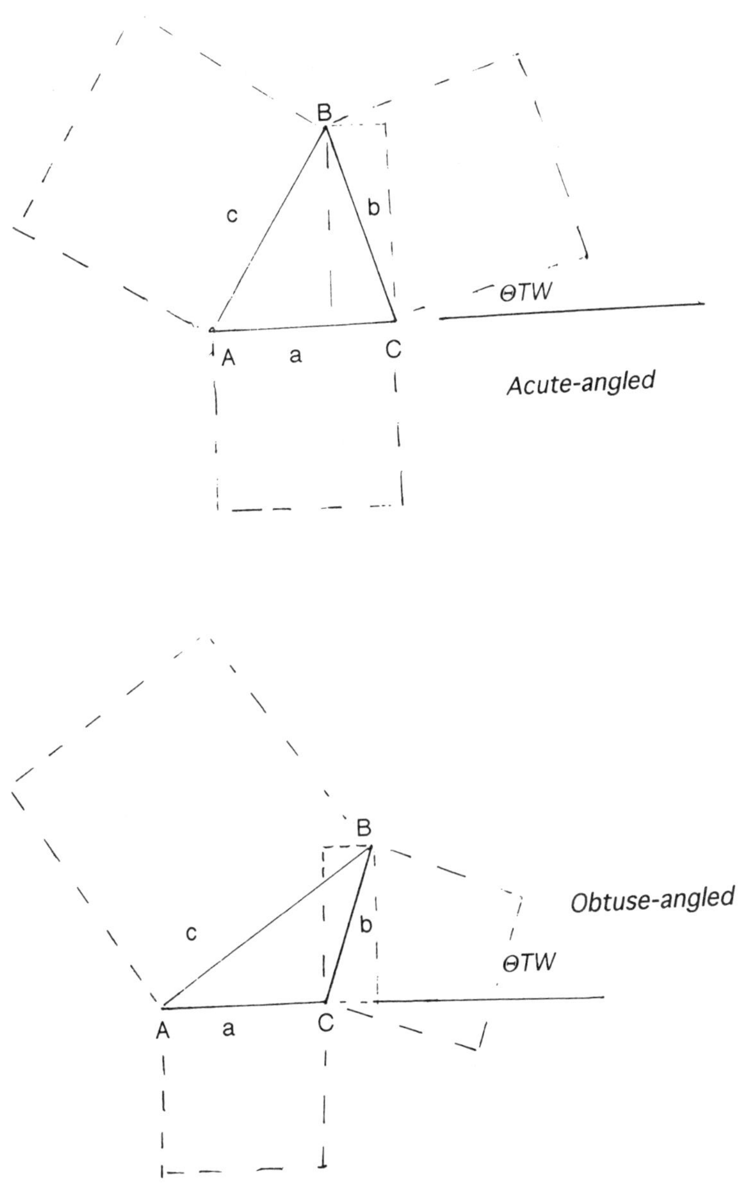


Figure I-1
Triangles for Euclid's Propositions

The law of cosines (p. 8 CRC *Standard Mathematical Tables, 20th edition*, CRC Press 1972, Cleveland) in current analytic terms is represented by Equations (I-1) and (I-2) below. Line lengths, *a*, *b*, and *c*, and angles *A*, *B*, and *C* correspond to those in Figure I-1.

$$c^2 = a^2 + b^2 - 2ab \cos C \tag{I-1}$$

$$A + B + C = 180° \tag{I-2}$$

Analytic Solutions for the Euclidian Triangle for *ß* in terms of ⊝*TW*, *VB* and *VTW*, with

a = *VTW*, C = 180° - ⊝*TW*, and b = *VB*, c = *VAW*, and B = *ß*, are:

for *ß* < 90°

$$ß = ß1 =$$
ASIN(sin⊝*TW*×1 ÷ √(1 + (*VB*/ *VTW*)$^2$-2(*VB*/ *VTW*)cos(180°-⊝*TW*)))
$$\tag{I-3}$$

for *ß* > 90°

$$ß = 180° - ß1. \tag{I-4}$$

A *ß1* check [from Milgrim (1993)] is,

$$ß1 = ATAN (VTW \sin⊝TW ÷ (VTW \cos ⊝TW + VB)) \tag{I-5}$$

# Appendix II - The Blank Page

Sometime in 1988/89 I sat down in front of a blank page and wrote what I thought was true about the sailboat in motion. It could not, with conventional thinking, or current advanced understandings explain what I had observed earlier.

What I had observed sometime earlier was that two high-speed catamarans, one 32 ft long, the other 68 ft long, both well manned and well sailed, had sailed in the same wind around the same course, neck and neck, and had finished within seconds of each other. In other words, they sailed at nearly the same speed in the same wind for a long period of time over the same smooth seas. How could this be? The much longer cat with much more sail area should have been much faster, should have pierced the finish line much sooner than the shorter catamaran.

For some time, about two weeks, I concentrated on trying to explain and understand the startling observed result between the two fast cats. I stared at what I had written on the blank page and tried using all my university-obtained and post-university-obtained knowledge to explain the phenomenon observed. Each time I considered it, the logical conclusion came out, "The big cat should have been faster by a lot of time." So I spent two more days staring at the three relations on the paper I thought were true, but not with any more pre-conclusions as to what they said or to their interpretation; I had cleared my mind. On about the third day in the morning, I looked at the paper again and an idea came to my head—what if there were a function that modified the balance in equation one? What if there was a modulating function composed of heeling moment available and righting moment required, a ratio of these two that was controlling and existed? Then what? Okay, I said, what is it and how is it to be applied? From then on (after defining the modulating function), the leaps were not as large and were cautiously made along the lines of if-this-is-true, then what, and some early predictions were made and the understanding of the theory developed with some knowledge of the performance of real boats from my files and commissioned work, the commissioners not knowing everything that was afoot, but knowing I was excited about something and could produce polar charts in several winds for their boats!

The discovery didn't just happen; it took a willingness to be open minded and seek for a more complete truth than what was the conventional at the time regarding how nature works its wonder with an object (a physical one at that) and even for one that has been around a long time.

The blank page beginning is shown in Figure II-1. What was first written on the blank page is shown in Figure II-2. The development of the method of the free modulating function and the general theory of Chapter 3 is the result of a willingness to take a look at an old problem with fresh eyes and mind and pursue an idea.

Figure II-1
The Blank Page

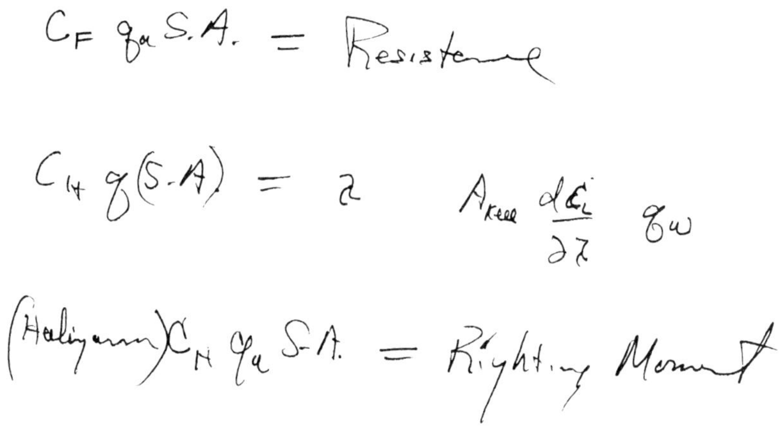

$C_F\, q_a\, S.A. = \text{Resistance}$

$C_H\, q(S.A.) = \partial \quad A_{keel}\, \frac{dC_L}{\partial \lambda}\, q_w$

$(\text{Heeling arm})\, C_H\, q_a\, S.A. = \text{Righting Moment}$

Figure II-2
What Was Written on the Blank Page

# Appendix III - Raw Wind Force Charts

Raw Wind Forces (*RAWF*) Charts for some sailing possibilities are in this section. *RAWF* versus boat speed, *VB* (knots) for true wind speeds, *VTW* of 5, 10, 15 and 20 knots, for several $C_D/C_L$ ratios and *B/H* = 0.4 at true wind angles, $\Theta TW$, of 45°, 90°, and *B/H* = 0.2 at true wind angles, $\Theta TW$, of 135° and 165°, are presented. Since *RAWF* is linear in *B/H*, other curves for specific boats sailing at less *B/H*, or more *B/H*, can be drawn directly on the charts and used as driving force per pound displacement curves.

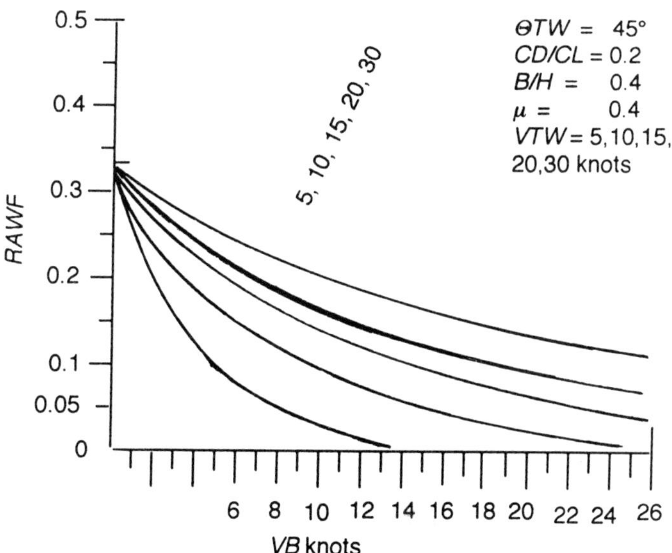


RAWF Chart 1
$\Theta TW$ = 45°, *VTW* = 5, 10, 15, 20, and 30 knots,
$C_D/C_L$ = 0.2, *B/H* = 0.4, $\mu$ = 0.4

The same is true for $1/(2\mu)$. The Charts are based on the general theory of Chapter 3. [See (5)**, (6)***, and (8) **** in Chapter 3.] The beauty of the theory and the charts is that any resistance curve, however produced, can be driven through the charts to produce a predicted speed for the corresponding vessel, craft or "sailing object." These charts are best used when boat speeds are such that the apparent wind angle, ß, is equal to or less than 90°. See the end of Chapter 3 and Appendix IV.

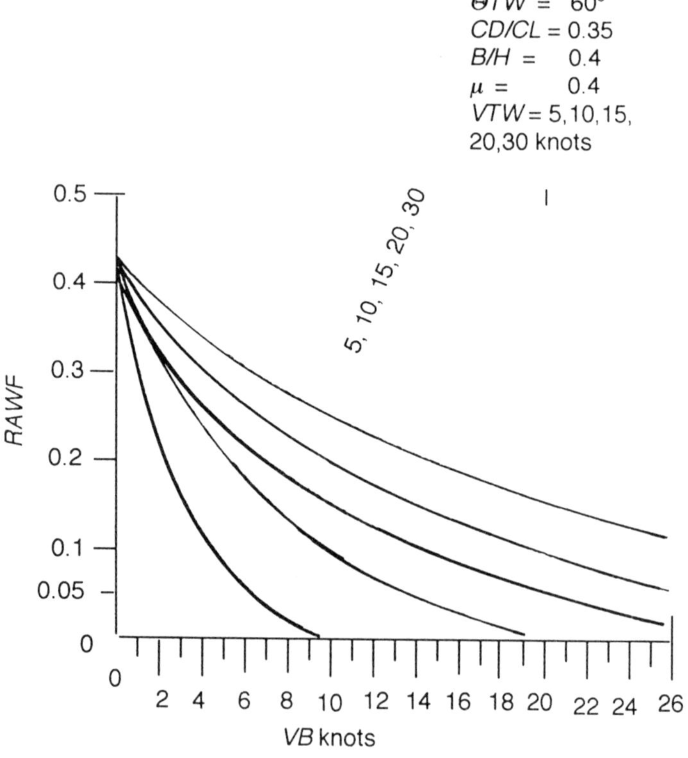


RAWF Chart 2
$\Theta TW = 60°$, $VTW = 5, 10, 15, 20$, and 30 knots,
$C_D/C_L = 0.35$, $B/H = 0.4$, $\mu = 0.4$

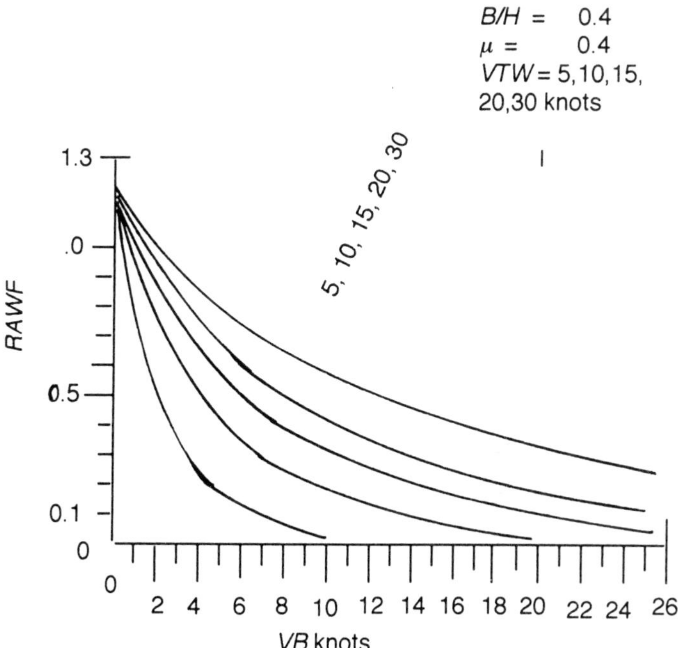



RAWF Chart 3
ΘTW = 90°, VTW = 5, 10, 15, 20, and 30 knots,
$C_D$ /$C_L$ = 0.4, B/H = 0.4, μ = 0.4

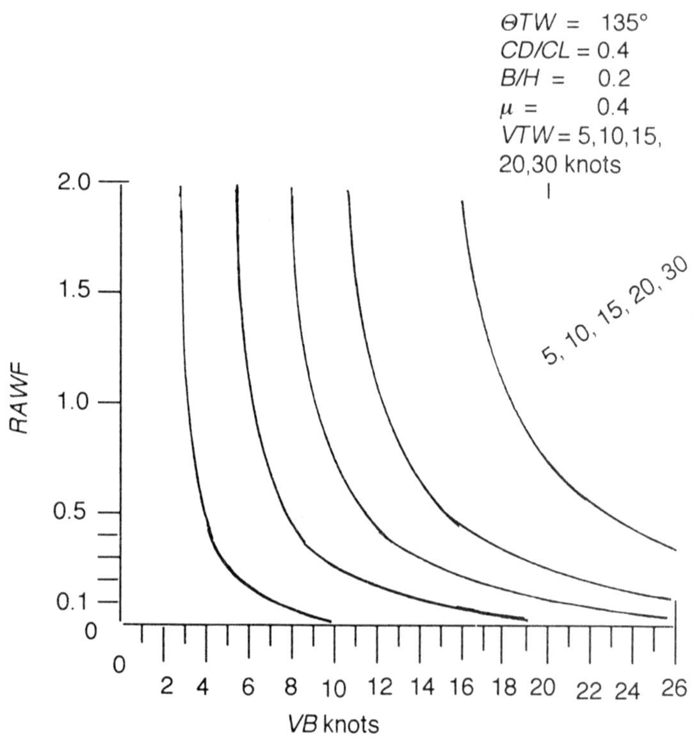


*RAWF* Chart 4
ΘTW = 135°, VTW = 5, 10, 15, 20, and 30 knots,
$C_D/C_L$ = 0.4, B/H = 0.2, μ = 0.4

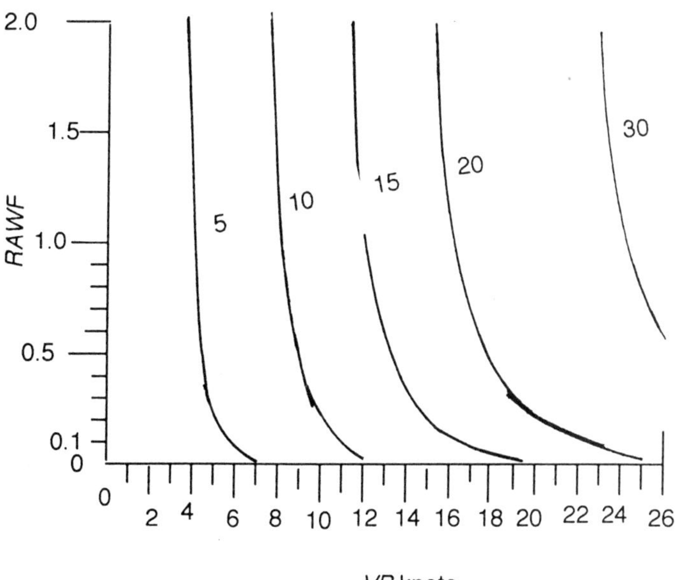


RAWF Chart 5
$\Theta TW$ = 165°, VTW = 5, 10, 15, 20, and 30 knots,
$C_D/C_L$ = 1.0, B/H = 0.2, $\mu$ = 0.4

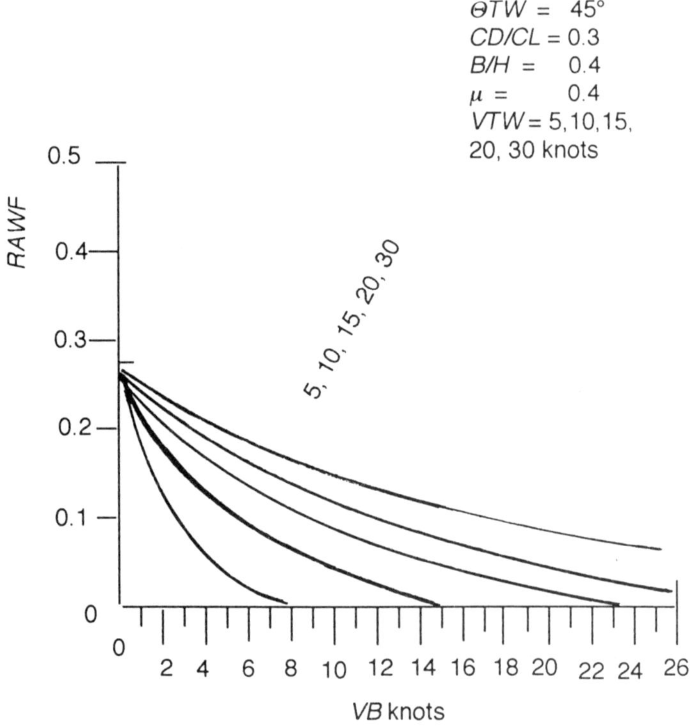


RAWF Chart 6
$\Theta TW = 45°$, $VTW = 5, 10, 15, 20$, and 30 knots,
$C_D/C_L = 0.3$, $B/H = 0.4$, $\mu = 0.4$

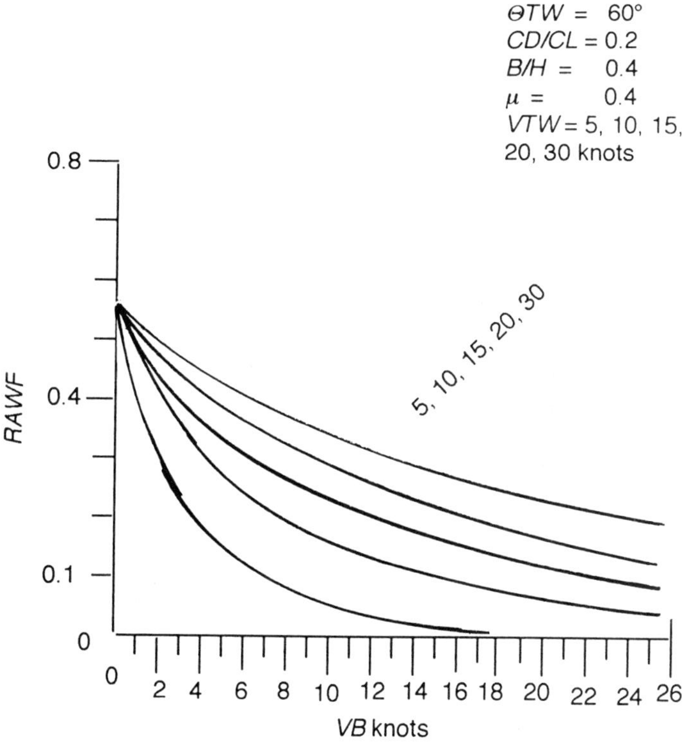


*RAWF* Chart 7
ΘTW = 60°, VTW = 5, 10, 15, 20, and 30 knots,
$C_D/C_L = 0.2$, B/H = 0.4, $\mu = 0.4$

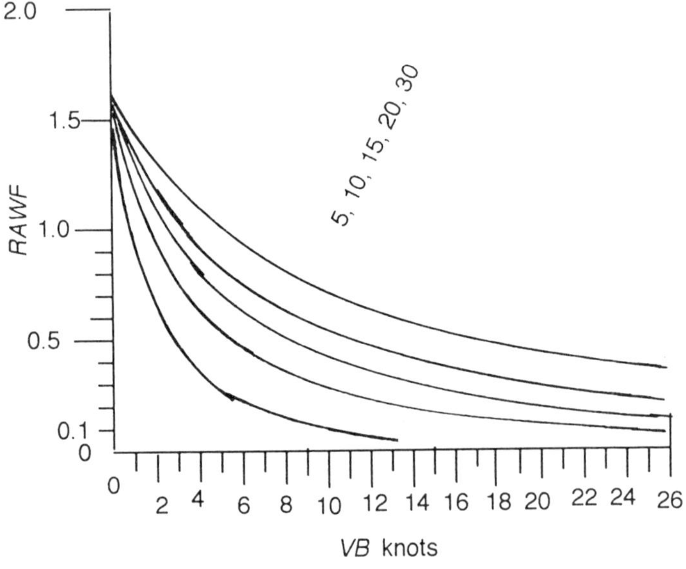


*RAWF* Chart 8
$\Theta TW$ = 90°, *VTW* = 5, 10, 15, 20, and 30 knots,
$C_D / C_L$ = 0.3, *B/H* = 0.4, $\mu$ = 0.4

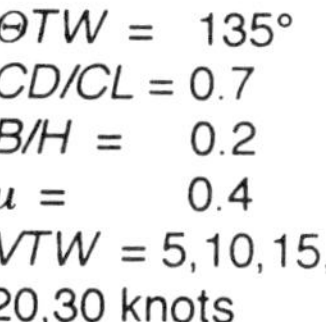


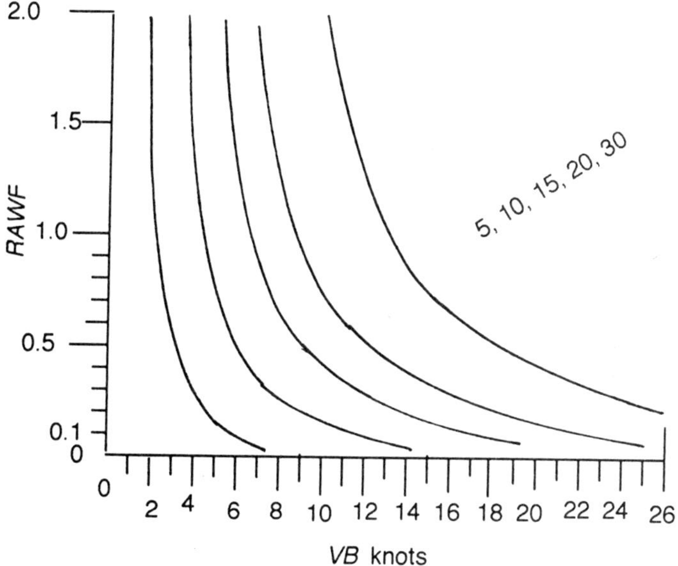


*RAWF* Chart 9
ΘTW = 135°, VTW = 5, 10, 15, 20, and 30 knots,
$C_D/C_L$ = 0.7, B/H = 0.2, $\mu$ = 0.4

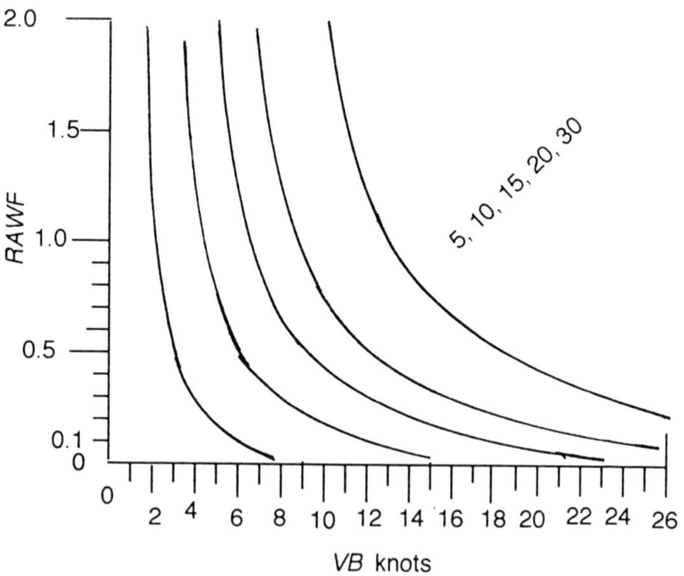


*RAWF* Chart 10
ΘTW = 165°, VTW = 5, 10, 15, 20, and 30 knots,
$C_D/C_L$ = 3.0, B/H = 0.2, μ = 0.4

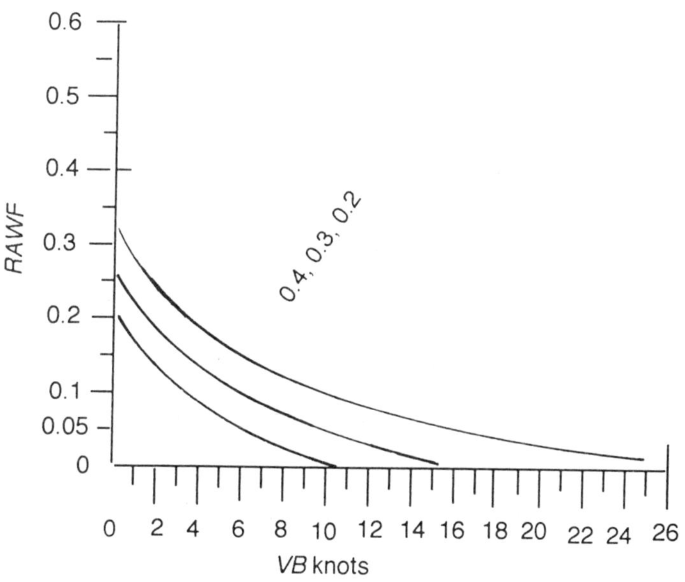


*RAWF* Chart 11
$\Theta TW = 45°$, $VTW = 10$ knots
$C_D/C_L = 0.2, 0.3, 0.4$, $B/H = 0.4$, $\mu = 0.4$

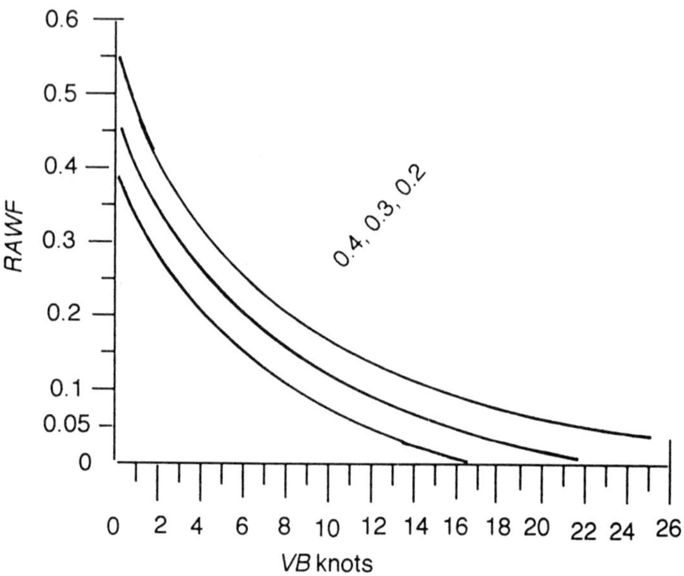


*RAWF* Chart 12
$\Theta TW = 60°$, $VTW = 10$ knots,
$C_D /C_L = 0.2, 0.3, 0.4$, $B/H = 0.4$, $\mu = 0.4$

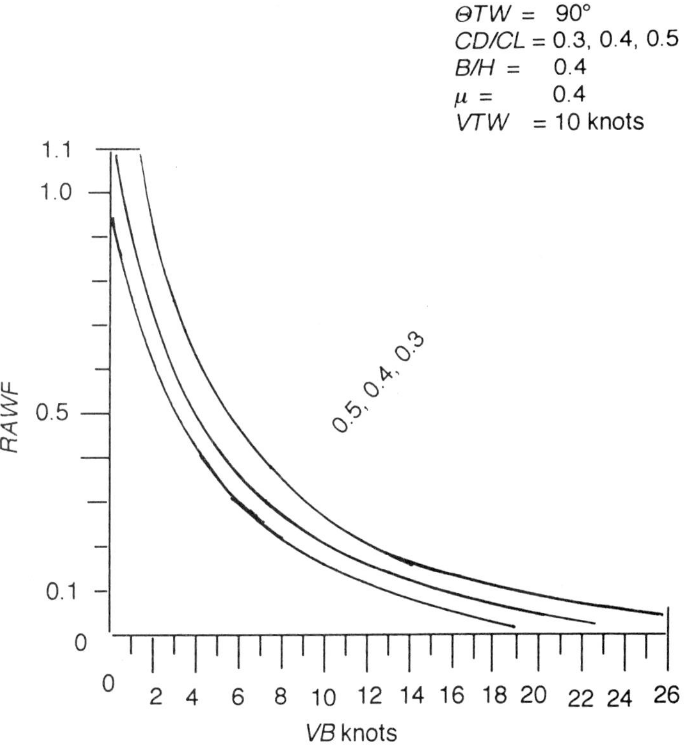


*RAWF* Chart 13
$\Theta TW = 90°$, $VTW = 10$ knots,
$C_D/C_L = 0.3, 0.4, 0.5$, $B/H = 0.4$, $\mu = 0.4$

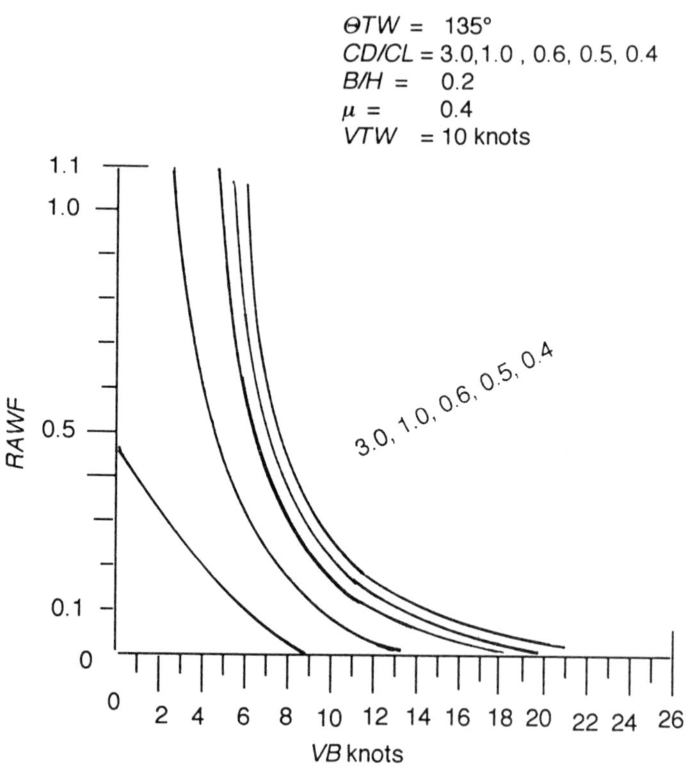


*RAWF* Chart 14
$\Theta TW = 135°$, $VTW = 10$ knots,
$C_D/C_L = 3.0, 1.0, 0.4, 0.5, 0.6$, $B/H = 0.2$, $\mu = 0.4$

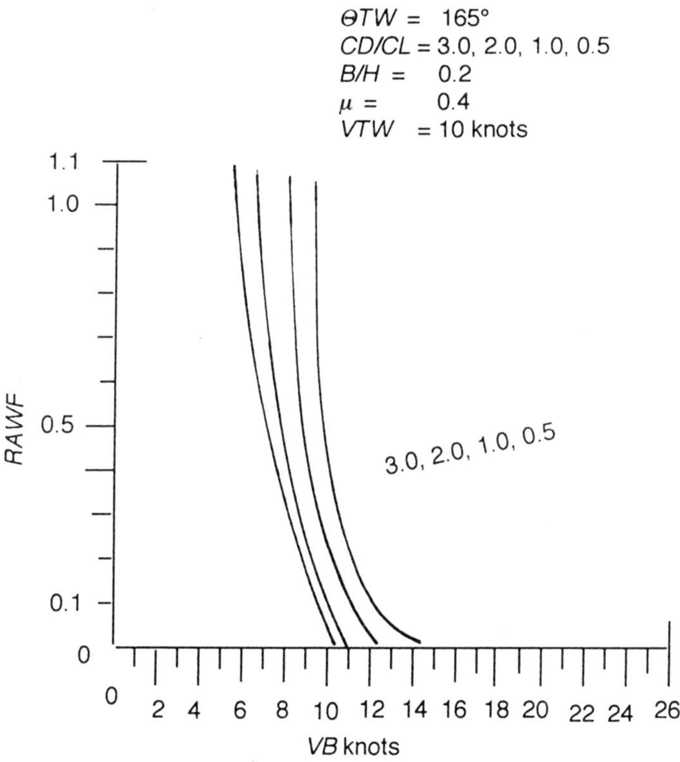



*RAWF* Chart 15
ΘTW = 165°, *VTW* = 10 knots,
$C_D/C_L$ = 0.5, 1.0, 2.0, 3.0, B/H = 0.2, μ = 0.4

A special note for iceboats and land sailors: These RAWF charts can be used  equally for iceboats and land sailing craft.  To use them for iceboats and landsailors convert *VB*  and *VTW* to miles per hour (mph).

# Appendix IV - Conventional Driving Force Coefficients, $C_F$

At boat speeds where $|C_H| \to 0$ or ß is greater than 90°, it may be preferable to use $C_F\, q_a\, (S.A./\Delta)$ for driving force per pound displacement representations instead of *RAWF* of Appendix III. Figure IV-1 presents boat's speeds corresponding to $|C_H| \to 0$ for a range of *⊖TWs* and a range of $C_D/C_L$ with *VTW* = 10 knots. (In Figure IV-1, *VB* at $C_D/C_L = 0$ corresponds to ß = 90°.) Figure IV-2 presents drive force coefficients, $C_F$ for *⊖TW* = 135° and a range of $C_D/C_L$ and $C_L$, and *VTW* = 10 knots. Figure IV-3 presents driving force coefficients, $C_F$ for *⊖TW* = 165° and a range of $C_D/C_L$ and $C_L$, and *VTW* = 10 knots. (Note that $C_F$ in Figures IV-2 and IV-3 is linear in $C_L$ since $C_F = C_L(\Omega)\,[\sin ß - (C_D/C_L)\,(\Omega)\,\cos ß])$.

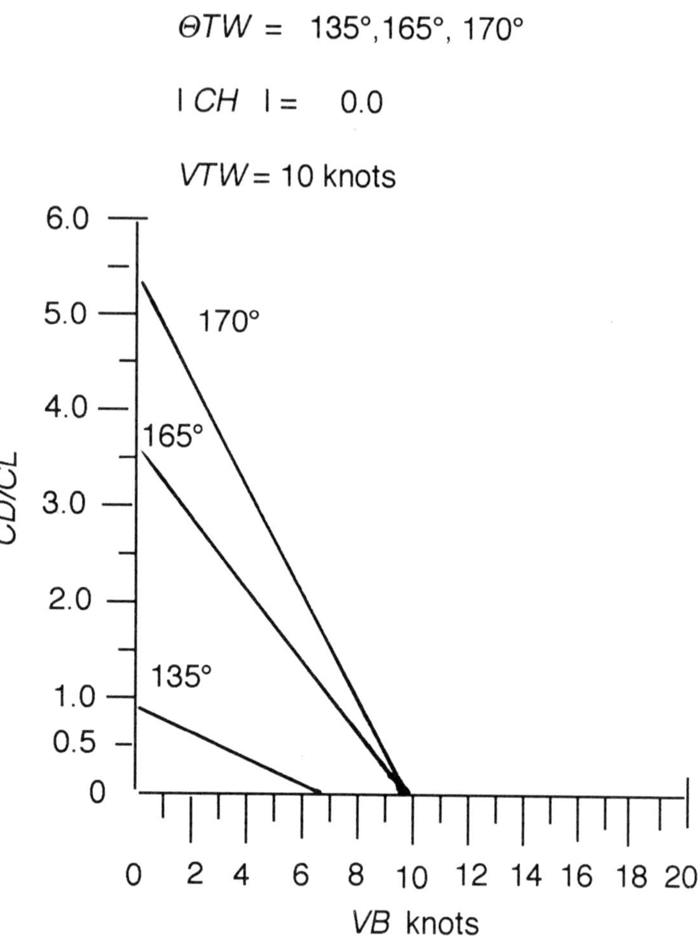


Figure IV-1
Boat Speeds, *VB*, Corresponding to | *CH* | -> 0
for a Range of *ΘTWs* and a Range of $C_D/C_L$. *VTW* = 10 Knots.

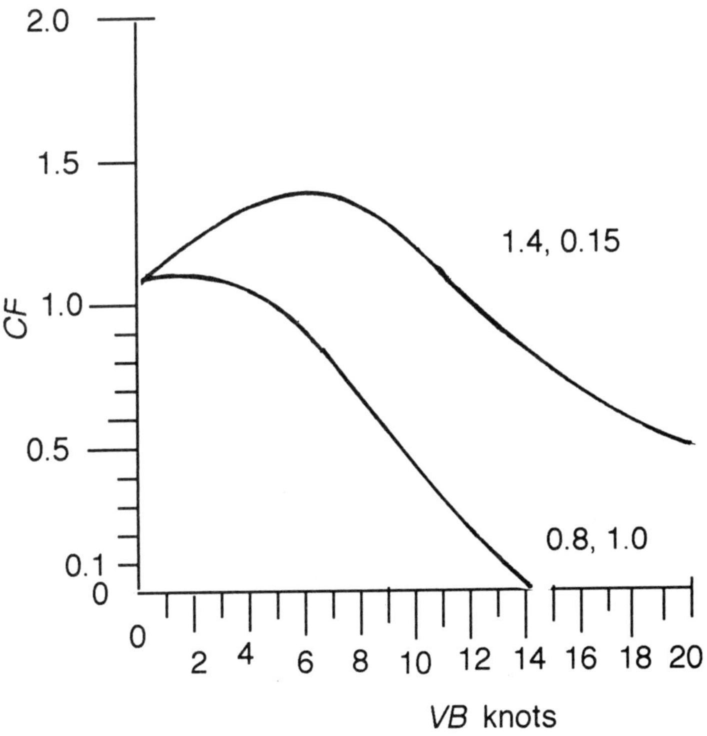



Figure IV-2

$C_F$ for $\Theta TW$ = 135° and a Range of $C_D/C_L$ and $C_L$, and $VTW$ = 10 knots.

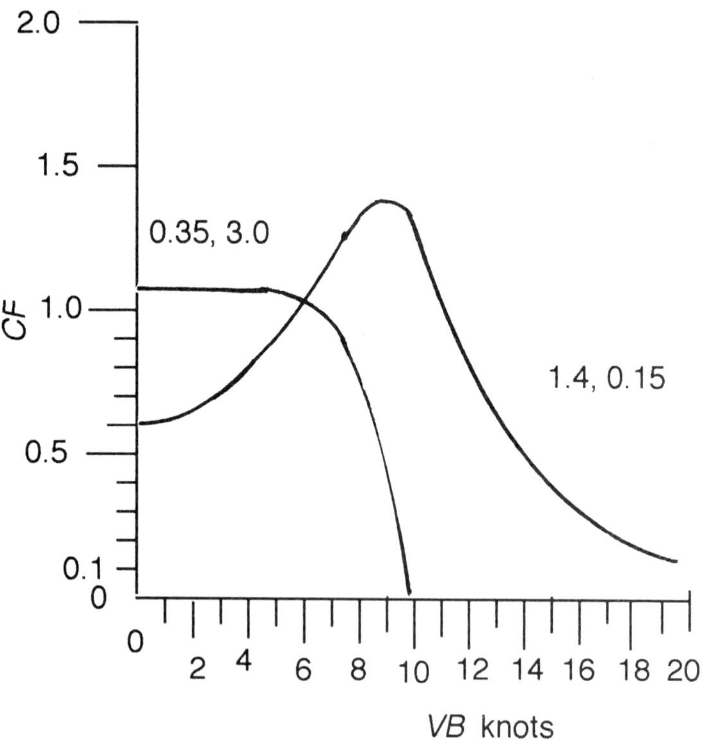


Figure IV-3

$C_F$ for $\Theta TW = 165°$ and a Range of $C_D/C_L$ and $C_L$, and $VTW = 10$ knots.

# Appendix V - Table of Historical Dates

It is the wish of the author to acknowledge that many of the concepts on which the general theory stands are based on the works of predecessors and taught in modern schools and colleges. For example, two of Euclid's propositions are reviewed in Appendix I. The approximate dates for these concepts and others, and their originators are listed in Table IV-1. The date of the first record of the general theory primitive result for *RAWF* (see Chapter 3) is in an unpublished copyrighted manuscript by Selness, "From Out of the Fifth Dimension, Into the Third and Onto the Fourth" (1989). (See this text, Chapter 5, page 75.) The dates in the table are from Smith (1953), Boyer (1968), Casson (1971), or Hoerner (1965).

| 4000 BC | first recorded image of boats (C) |
| 3000 BC | use of wheeled vehicles (B) |
| 1032 BC | first historical record of rules for Chinese currency by weight (S) |
| *540 BC | pythagorean arithmetic and geometry (S) (B) |
| 427 BC | birth of Plato (B) |
| *300 BC | Euclids Elements, law of cosines (S) (B) |
| *225 BC | Archimedes, geometry, mechanics (S) |
| 212 BC | Death of Archimedes (B) |
| 250 AD | Diophantis (B) |
| 275 AD | Diophantis, positive number analysis, theory of numbers, algebra (B) |
| 1270 AD | Wm of Moerbeke translated Archimedes (B) |
| 1482 AD | First printed Euclid (B) |
| 1564 AD | Birth of Galileo (B) |
| 1629 AD | Femats method of maxima and minima (B) |
| 1637 AD | Desartes Discours de la Methode Analyltic Geometry (S) (B) |
| 1642 AD | Birth of Newton (B) |
| *1680 AD | Sir Issac Newton. Fluxional calculas, physics (S) |
| 1687 AD | Newton Principia (B) |
| 1743 AD | D'Alembert. Traite de dynamique (B) |
| 1780 AD | Lagrange (S) |
| 1788 AD | Lagrange Mecanique analytique (B) |
| 1810 AD | William Froude born, the free surface similarity law is named after him (H) |
| *1873 AD | Maxwell, physical qualities of physical objects can be regarded as numbers or points. (B) |
| 1881 AD | Von karman, Theodore, born (B) |
| 1875 AD | Prandtl, Ludwing, born (B) |
| *1906 | Lanchester- Prandtl (H) Wing Theory, Lift and Drag Concepts |

Chronological Table after: Smith (1953) = S, Boyer (1968) = B, Casson (1971) = C, Hoerner(1965) = H

Table IV-1

Chronological Table of Historical Dates
for Some Concepts (*) upon Which the General Theory Stands

# Glossary of Terms

| | |
|---|---|
| $a$ | Subscript denoting air |
| $arm$ | Righting arm associated with righting moment available |
| $A_{lateral}$ | Lateral area |
| $A_{frontal}$ | Frontal area |
| $A_{frontalhull}$ | Frontal area of hull |
| $A_{keel}$ | Keel area (lateral, one side only) |
| $A_{ref}$ | Reference area (frontal area of keel or hull) |
| $AGK$ | Aspect ratio, geometric |
| $AR_{eff}$ | Effective aspect ratio, for the keel, often $< 2\ ARGK$ |
| $ARGK$ | Aspect ratio, geometric, for the keel = (span$^2$ ÷ lateral area of keel, one side), $ARGK = T^2/A_{keel}$ |
| $AWF$ | Available Wind Force |
| $B$ | Beam of a catamaran or equivalent catamaran beam |
| $B/H$ | Catamaran beam-to-mast-height ratio or equivalent catamaran beam-to-mast-height ratio |
| $B/H$ | Theory parameter result |
| $B/H_{equivalent}$ | Equivalent $B/H$ for use with $RAWF$ and $AWF$ |
| $C_D$ | Drag force coefficient of the air |
| $C_D/C_L$ | Ratio of drag force coefficient of the air-to-lift force coefficient of the air |
| $C_F$ | Driving force coefficient of the air |
| $C_H$ | Heeling force coefficient |
| $C_F/C_H$ | Ratio of driving force coefficient to heeling force coefficient |
| $C_L$ | Lift force coefficient of the air |
| $C_{dfrontal}$ | Frontal area associated drag coefficient |
| $C_{fric}(Rn)$ | Coefficient of friction as a function of Reynolds number |
| $C_{Fric}$ | Frictional coefficient = 0.075 ÷ (log $Rn$ -2)^2 per International Towing Tank Conference (ITTC) |
| $CA$ | A correction factor for friction coefficient for the new vessel sometimes taken as 0.0004 or zero |
| $C_{dattached}$ | Coefficient of drag with attached flow, frontal area |
| $C_{dfully\ separated}$ | Coefficient of drag with fully separated flow, frontal area |
| $d$ | Draft, keel depth |

| | |
|---|---|
| $F_{adf}$ | Driving force of the air |
| $F_{ahf}$ | Heeling, sideways pulling force of the air |
| $F_{awindage}$ | Windage drag resistance on topsides |
| $F_{ahf} \times \mu H$ | Righting moment required for a sailboat |
| $F_{v}$ | Volume Froude number $= VB \div (\sqrt{g} \times \textbf{v}^{1/3})$ |
| $F_{whf}$ | Heeling, sideways force of the water opposite to $F_{ahf}$ |
| $F_{wrf}$ | Resisting force of the water opposite to $F_{adf}$ |
| $\underline{F}_{wrf}$ | Resisting force of the water for available wind forces |
| $F_{windage}$ | Windage drag |
| $F_{indkeel}$ | Induced drag of the keel |
| $"g"$ | Acceleration of gravity force |
| $H$ | Mast height above deck |
| $L$ | Length; waterline length or % of waterline length |
| $LH\ side$ | Left hand side |
| $L/\textbf{v}^{1/3}$ | Length to volume to the one third power ratio |
| $m_{i}$ | Mass |
| $M_{ahf}$ | Heeling moment from the sideways forces of the air |
| $M_{wrf}$ | Righting moment from all sources, but primarily those related to water flows |
| $P,\ P_{i}$ | Point |
| $q_{a}$ | Kinetic energy density of air $= 1/2\ \rho_a\ VAW^2$ |
| $q_{w}$ | Kinetic energy density of water $= 1/2\ \rho_w\ VB^2$ |
| $R_{T}$ | Total resistance |
| $\underline{R}_{T}$ | Same as $\underline{F}_{wrf}$, for use with available wind forces |
| $\underline{R}_{Tmin}$ | Minimum total resistance for use with available wind forces |
| $R_{up}$ | Upright resistance of the hull |
| $R_{app}$ | Appendage resistance |
| $R_{appatt}$ | Appendage drag-resistance from attached flow |
| $R_{appsep}$ | Appendage drag-resistance from separated flow |
| $R_{h}$ | Hull heeled resistance |
| $R_{induced}$ | Induced drag-resistance |
| $R_{indkeel}$ | Induced drag-resistance from flow on the keel |
| $R_{wave}$ | Wave resistance |
| $R_{friction}$ | Frictional resistance |
| $R_{hullsep}$ | Separated flow drag on the hull |
| $R_{correction}$ | Towing tank data correction |
| $R_{windage}$ | Resistance from windage drag |

| | |
|---|---|
| *RAWF* | Raw wind force (pound force per pound displacement) |
| *RH side* | Right hand side |
| *Rn* | Reynolds number = $VB \times L \div$ kinematic viscous coefficient for the fluid approximately equals 4.59 x $F_v \times (L/\forall^{1/3}) \times \forall^{1/3} \times 10\text{\textasciicircum}5$ ($\forall$ in $ft^3$) |
| *S.A.* | Sail area, *S.A.* = planform sail area |
| *S.A./Δ* | Sail area to displacement ratio |
| *source pair* | *VTW* and *VB* |
| *T* | Span of the keel |
| $t_i$ | Time at instant *i* |
| *WSSA* | World Speed Sailing Association |
| *windage* | Windage drag |
| $\forall$ | Volume displacement corresponding to Archimedes displacement |
| *VAW* | Speed or velocity of apparent wind from the source pair |
| *VB*, $VB_i$ | Boat speed, boat velocity; there is always a course direction associated with boat speed |
| *-VB* | Flow of water relative to the boat |
| $VB_{equilibrium}$ | Equilibrium boat speed |
| *VTW* | Speed or velocity of the true wind |
| *W* | Weight, often the same as Δ |
| $W_i = m_i\, g_i$ | Newtonian definition of weight force |
| *W.S.* | Wetted surface |
| $W.S./\forall^{2/3}$ | Wetted surface of new vessel to volume to the 2/3 power of a vessel; it depends on the hull form and is often between 2 and 3 |
| *zf* | Freeboard height (distance between water level and main deck edge of boat) |
| *2armi/H* | Equivalent *B/H* for a monohull or any sailing vessel |
| *α* | Angle of attack |
| *ß* | Apparent wind angle from the source pair |
| *δ* | Trim angle for sail from boat centerline |
| Δ | Weight displacement of vessel |
| Δ x *armi* | Righting Moment Available = displacement times arbitrary righting arm |
| *η Fadf* | Modulating function times driving forces of the air |

| $\eta$ | Modulating function, Righting Moment Available ÷ Righting Moment Required |
| $\lambda$ | Leeway angle, angle of attack of water on keel or hull |
| $\mu$ | Fraction of heeling arm to mast height ratio |
| $\mu H$ | Heeling arm from heeling forces of the air |
| $\Theta_H$ | Heeling angle |
| $\Theta TW$ | True wind angle (for course of $VB$) |
| $\Theta TW$ | Angle of boat speed direction to the true wind direction |
| $\Theta_{Hmax}$ | Maximum heeling angle |
| $\rho_a$ | Density of air |
| $\rho_w$ | Density of water |
| $\Sigma$ | Flat surface |
| $\Omega$ | Angle of attack of air flow on the sail rig for $VAW$ |
| $=$ | Equals sign |
| $->$ | "Goes to" |
| $=>$ | Implies |
| $\updownarrow$ | Difference |
| $cms^{-1}$ | Centimeters per second |
| $ms^{-1}$ | Meters per second |
| knots | Nautical miles per hour |
| mg | Milligrams |
| lbs | Pounds |
| ft | Feet |
| $\delta(F/\Delta)$ | Difference between driving force and resistance force $= (F_{raw/\Delta} - R_T/\Delta)$ |
| $VB_j$ | $VB_i + \delta VB_i$ |
| $\delta VB_i$ | Increment of speed |
| $i$ | Instant $t_i$ |
| crosswind | $\Theta TW = 90°$ |
| downwind | $\Theta TW = 180°$ |
| above crosswind | $\Theta TW < 90°$ |
| higher than downwind | $\Theta TW < 180°$ |
| \| \| | Absolute value |

# Notes

# Annotated Bibliography
## (Reverse Chronological Order)


Day, Alexander H., and Doctors, Lawrence J. "Resistance Optimization of Displacement Vessels on the Basis of Principal Parameters," *Journal of Ship Research*, December 1997, vol. 41, No. 4.
Calculates resistance per pound displacement for minimum resistance hull forms with wave and frictional resistance for the Wigley hull form. Data compares closely to minimum resistance from other sources.

Blount, Donald, and Bartee, Robert J. "Design of Propulsion Systems for High-Speed Craft," *Marine Technology*, October 1997, Vol 34, Number 4.
Includes resistance-per-pound displacement for a class of hulls and windage factor for topsides.

IYRU (International Yacht Racing Union)/ World Speed Record Council 1995/1997, Royal Yachting Association, Hants, England "1995/97 World Sailing Speed Record Rules Including Record Rules for Individually Attempted Passage Records."
Sets down rules for recording official speed passage records for sailboats. Contains the current speed records to date for specific sailboats.

Ellison, Michael. "25 Years of Sail," *Sail Magazine*, January 1995.
Describes the high-speed vessels, their speeds, and the conditions in which they made them.

Oliver, Peter J. *Equivalence, Invariant, and Symmetry*, Cambridge University Press, 1995.
Includes Cartan's "technique of the graph." Includes global equivalence. Has a definition for total derivative. Discuses invariant functions and rotations. Begins in the introduction with "the fundamental equivalence problem."

Pickthall, Barry. "Australian Fast Lady Out to Break 50 Knots," *The Times*, London, 12 Oct 1993.
Describes the vessel type and record voyages of *Yellow Pages-Endeavor*, current speed record holder. The description is

used to make speed predictions from the theory for the vessels.

Milgrim, Jerome H. "Naval Architecture Technology Used in Winning the 1992 America's Cup Match", Society of Naval Architects and Marine Engineers (SNAME) Trans, 1993.
   Excellent paper for describing the sailboat problem in general. Ignores leeway angle in setting the three defining general equations of motion to describe the sailboat. Some useful data is included despite attempts to not make clear specific performance factors in this scientific paper.

Van Oossanen, Peter. "Predicting the Speed of Sailing Yachts," Society of Naval Architects and Marine Engineers (SNAME) Trans. 1993.
   Summarizes the two iterative-algorithmic-computer based models currently in use as theories for sailboat performance predictions. How detailed can the study of a sailboat be? This paper identifies and defines more than 90 variables as parts of the complexities of the theories in use. (In contrast, the general theory uses far fewer variables for predictive purposes and is noniterative or only one iteration is required.)

Long, Russel. "A Long Shot," *Sail Magazine*, June 1992.
   Describes the trifoil-hydrofoil sailboat *Longshot* and its high speed, record-setting voyages. (The information is used to identify the *B/H* ratio for the theory application).

Brown, Stuart F. "Breaking the Limits of Sailboat Speed," *Yachting Magazine*, April 1991.
   Describes high-speed sailing vessels and their speeds and conditions in which the speeds were made to the date of 1991.

Smith, Bernard. *Sailloons and Fliptackers: The Limits to High Speed Sailing*. Washington, D.C., AIAA, 1989.
   Presents a theory of sailing limits based on drag angles and one equation of equilibrium for an idealistic aerofoil-hydrofoil craft. Assumes limiting drag angles and seizes on the drag angle results of Marchaj to define speed limits for sailboats. Does not take righting moment into account. Presents a section on the evolutionary origins of the sailboat that depicts regional development of rigs for Oceana, Eastern Asia, and Western branches of

European development. (Smith's result predicts limits that sharply contrast to those of the general theory.)

Crick, Francis. *What Mad Pursuit, A Personal View of Scientific Discovery*, New York: Basic Books, 1988.
Presents views on the process of discovery in general and the character of DNA in particular (1953-1966) by Crick and Jim Watson. Epilogue of later years is very interesting in terms of consciousness and the other.

PNA. *Principles of Naval Architecture Vol.II, Resistance, Propulsion, and Vibration*, SNAME, 1988.
A comprehensive volume of a three-volume set that sets the understandings of the ship hull and appendages that are accepted today for propeller driven vessels.

Theisen, Wilfred. "Euclid, Relativity, and Sailing," *Historia Mathematica* 11, 1984, p.81-85.
Claims ships led Euclid to consider relative motion and optics in his applied mathematics using triangles.

Hazen, George S. "A Model of Sail Aerodynamics for Diverse Rig Types," *The New England Sailing Yacht Symposium*, collected papers, March 22, 1980.
Presents drag and lift coefficients for several rigs versus apparent wind angle $\beta$.

Kerwin, J. E. "A Velocity Prediction Program for Ocean Racing Yachts Revised to June 1978," July, Report #78-11 (1986 Coefficients). H. Irving Pratt Ocean R&E, Handicapping Project, MIT, 1986-1978.
The current basis for the Measurement Handicap System for offshore sailing yachts. Requires exact knowledge of the hull shape and by iterative procedures forces an approximate solution to the three coupled equations of motion. Contains tables and charts of data from controlled experiments for a range of hull shapes.

Letcher, John S. Jr. "Optimal Performance of Ships Under Combined Power and Sail," *Journal of Ship Research*, vol. 26, no. 3, September 1982.
Most recent paper in the *Journal of Ship Research* on the

subject matter. Uses sail coefficients for Dynaship type vessels. Uses frontal area as a reference area in the theory presented. Does not address righting moment. Calls the sailboat problem "complex." Is an extension of his 1976 theory.

Savitsky, D., and Gore, J.L. "Reevaluation of the Planing Hull Form," *Journal of Hydronautics*, vol. 14, no. 2, April 1980.
Results of tests on semi-planing hulls are presented as resistance in the form of resistance per pound displacement and Volume Froude number. This representation is used for resistance in the general theory.

Bradfield, W.S. "On the Design of Radical High Speed Sailing Vessels," *Marine Technology*, vol. 17, no. 1, January 1980.
Describes the design of specific sailing vessels that might make high speeds.

Norwood, Joseph Jr. *High Speed Sailing*, New York: Dodd, Mead, 1979.
Presents a unified theory that includes wave, hull form, and frictional drag theories for the hull and aerodynamic theories for the rig. Produces a single expression result for specific sailboats that does account for righting moment. Not in general use because the predicted speeds from Norwood's theory and the actual speeds attained differ by 25%-30%. Bases theory in part on ratio of boat speed to true wind speed result of the velocity triangle. Contains some useful data and references to other theories' results including a ratio of boat speed to true wind speed for specific boats extended from a true wind velocity of 10 knots to all true wind velocities. Uses a hull-afly approximation to define a limiting value of righting moment and speed for specific vessels.

Marchaj, C.A. *Aero-Hydrodynamics of Sailing*, New York: Dodd, Mead, 1979.
The most comprehensive work to date for sailboats that includes extensive aerodynamic and hydrodynamic theoretical results and empirical data for components of sailboats.

Curtiss H. C. "Upright Sailing Craft Performance and Optimum Speed to Windward," *Journal of Hydronautics*, vol. 11, no. 2, 1977.

The theory of a Princeton mathematician for upwind sailboat performance. Like most previous theories, it does not address overturning/righting moment in the theory.

Letcher, J. S., Jr. "Optimum Windward Performance of Sailing Craft," *Journal of Hydronautics*, vol. 10, no.4, October 1976.
A theory to predict the optimum upwind performance of a sailboat. Makes a conclusion from the theory results that drag to lift for the rig is of secondary importance for the optimization of upwind performance which is contrary to the basic drag angle model proved by Marchaj (1964).

Johnson, Peter. *Boating Facts and Feats*, New York: Sterling, 1976, pp. 22-23.
Sailboats, their descriptions, and passage achievements prior to 1976.

Scherer, Otto J. "Aerodynamics of High Performance Wing Sails," *Chesapeake Sailing Yacht Symposium*, SNAME section, 19 January 1974.
An early discussion of aerodynamic theory and presents test results for efficient sailboat rigs. Includes drag to lift data.

Kinney, Francis S. *Skene's Elements of Yacht Design,* 8th ed., New York: Dodd, Mead, 1973.
A treasure of information about designed sailboats. There is a polar chart for *Yankee Girl* and a section with calculations for *Pipe Dream. Waupi* is a first boat that I sailed on in 1959, long before sailing had become such a part of my life.

Milgram, J. H. *Sail Force Coefficients for Systematic Rig Variations*, SNAME T&R report R-10, 1971.
Sail force coefficients for rigs from general inverse aerodynamic theory. Relates the coefficients to the apparent wind velocity squared. These are still in use for approximate force coefficients for a variety of rigs.

Southworth, John Van Duyn. *War at Sea*, New York: Twayne, 1968. Four volumes.
Vol. 1, *The Ancient Fleets*, vol. 2, *The Age of Sail* and vol. 3, *The Age of Steam.* Part One, concern naval battles involving

sailing vessels, battle after battle.

Boyer, Carl B. *A History of Mathematics*, New York: John Wiley and Sons, 1968.

Explains difference between Euclidean and non-Euclidean geometry, p.588. Has a chronological history in an appendix. Has an index. A good source of early mathematics. Includes Archimedes of Syracuse.

Schlichting, Hermann. *Boundary-Layer Theory*, trans. J. Kestin, New York: McGraw Hill, 1968, 1960, and 1955.

Comprehensive work regarding frictional resistance as represented by boundary-layer theory.

Hoerner, S. F. *Fluid Dynamic Drag*. Self-published, Lib of Cong. #64-19666, 1965.

Presents formulae from empirical test results in wind tunnels and towing tanks for components in general. Presents drag in the form of "drag area." Also presents results for attached and separated flow drag from fluids flowing around a body. Presents drag results from theories.

Marchaj, C.A. *Sailing Theory and Practice*, New York: Dodd, Mead, 1964.

One of the first works to present wind tunnel test results on actual sailing rigs in a complete theory. Identifies and proves the basic drag angle theorem for the upright sailboat. This theorem is used by most contemporary theories to check iterative closure results for the equations of motion.

Herreshoff, Halsey C. "Hydrodynamics and Aerodynamics of the Sailing Yacht," SNAME Transactions, November 1964.

Test results of towed models at MIT. Includes resistance curves for some models upright and heeled.

Meyers, Hugo. "Theory of Sailing-With Applications to Modern Catamarans," *Marine Technology*, October 1964.

Theory attempts to combine a number of major factors into a single expression. Uses Davidson's "Gimcrack" sail coefficients.

Robinson, Bill, ed. *The Science of Sailing,* New York: Charles Scribner's Sons, 1961.
    Several articles relating to sailing. George B Moffat, Jr. article, "Centerboards and Rudders," places rudders and keels into the perspective of the racing sailor.

Smith, David Eugene. *History of Mathematics,* Volume I, New York: Dover Publications, 1958.
    Contains a chronological table in the context of other historical events. First copyrighted in 1923.

D. Phillips-Birt. *The Naval Architecture of Small Craft,* London: Hutchinson Scientific and Technical, 1957.
    Presents sail coefficients that are related to a ratio of boat speed to the true wind speed a sailboat sails in.

Morwood, John. *Sailing Aerodynamics,* Adlard Cole Limited, Southampton, in association with John de Graff, Inc, New York, 1954.
    This work addresses sail forces in terms of coefficients based on S.R. speed ratios and other factors that effect sail forces. One chapter addresses the evaluation of some ancient sailing rigs (e.g., ancient egyptian ship ca. 1260 BC) (p.67).

Davidson, Kennith S. M. "Some Experimental Studies of the Sailing Yacht," *Transactions of The Society of Naval Architects and Marine Engineers,* vol. 44, 1936.
    The first paper I ever read on the subject in 1975. It is a classic in that it produces sail force thrust coefficients from towing tank test results on sailboat hull models in a theory. The "gimcrack coefficients" were used until the early 1970s.

Other sources of technical information regarding sailing and sailboats can be found in:

AIAA Ancient Interface Yacht Symposiums
New England Sailing Yacht Symposiums
Chesapeake Sailing Yacht Symposiums
A.Y.R.S. publications (England)